PRAISE FOR

Seven Years in Tibet

~⌐

"It tells one of the grandest and most incredible adventure stories I have ever read, compounded of the infallibly exciting elements of mountain climbing, daring escapes, life in secret, forbidden Tibet, and encounters with extraordinary people."

—SANTHA RAMA RAU, *The New York Times Book Review*

"First there is the incredibly adventurous twenty-one-month trek across rugged mountain and desolate plain to the mysterious heart-land of Tibet; then the fascinating picture, rich in amazing detail, of life in Lhasa. . . . Final chapters draw an intimate portrait of the youthful Dalai Lama."

—*The Atlantic Monthly*

"Harrer's depiction of the [Dalai Lama as a youth], and of Tibetan culture, is a source that countless scholars, travelers, and others have drawn upon for four decades."

—D. J. R. BRUCKNER, *The New York Times*

"Mr. Harrer presents an intimate picture of Tibet, unlike that given by any other European, for no one ever had his opportunity to participate in the life of that strange city in the clouds."

—*New York Herald Tribune Book Review*

RETURN TO TIBET

JEREMY P. TARCHER/PUTNAM

a member of

PENGUIN PUTNAM INC.

New York

Return to Tibet

Tibet After the Chinese Occupation

HEINRICH HARRER

Translated from the German by

EWALD OSERS

Most Tarcher/Putnam books are available at special quantity discounts for bulk
purchases for sales promotions, fund-raising, and educational needs.
Special books or book excerpts also can be created to fit specific needs.
For details, write or telephone Putnam Special Markets, 200 Madison Avenue,
New York, NY 10016; (212) 951-8891.

JEREMY P. TARCHER/PUTNAM
a member of
Penguin Putnam Inc.
200 Madison Avenue
New York, NY 10016
www.penguinputnam.com

First American hardcover edition published by Schocken Books © 1985.
First American Trade Paperback Edition published by Jeremy P. Tarcher/
Putnam © 1998. Published by agreement with Schocken Books, Inc. Originally
published in Germany under the title *Wiedersehn mit Tibet,* copyright ©
Deutsche Ausgabe 1983 by Pinguin-Verlag.

Library of Congress Cataloging-in-Publication Data
Harrer, Heinrich, 1912–.
[Wiedersehn mit Tibet. English]
Return to Tibet : Tibet after the Chinese occupation / Heinrich
Harrer: translated from the German by Ewald Osers.
p.   cm.
Includes index.
ISBN 0-87477-925-1
1. Tibet (China)—History. I. Osers, Ewald.
DS786.H3313   1998   98-5345 CIP
951'.5—dc21

Book design by Deborah Kerner

Printed in the United States of America
2   4   6   8   10   9   7   5   3   1
This book is printed on acid-free paper. ∞

Contents

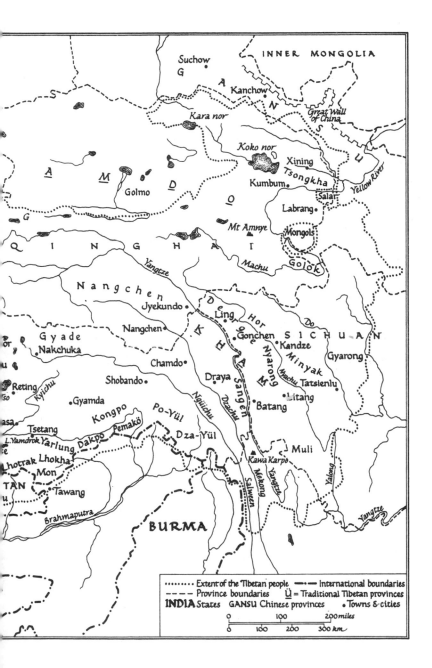

INNER MONGOLIA

Suchow
G

Kanchow

Great Wall
of China

Kara nor

Koko nor
Xining
Tsongkha
Kumbum·
Salar
Yellow River

A   M   D
Golmo

O

G

Labrang·

Mt Amnye ▲
Mongols

Q   I   N   G   H   A   I
Golok

Yangtze
Machu
Do

N a n g c h e n
Jyekundo·
De
Ling
Hor
Gonchen
S I C H U A N

Nangchen·
K
Nyarong
Kandze·
Minyak
Gyarong

G y a d e
·Nakchuka
Chamdo·
H
Draya·
Sangen
M
Machu Tatsienlu
·Litang

Reting
Kyichu
·Gyamda
Shobando·
A
Batang

Ngulchu
Dzachu

Tsetang
Kongpo
Po-Yül
Dza-Yül

L.Yamdrok
Yarlung
Dakpo
Pemakö
Muli

Lhotrak Lhokha
Mon
Kawa Karpo

TAN
·Tawang
Salween
Mekong
Yangtze
Yalong

Brahmaputra

BURMA
Yangtze

·········· Extent of the Tibetan people   —·— International boundaries
——— Province boundaries   Ṳ = Traditional Tibetan provinces
INDIA States   GANSU Chinese provinces   · Towns & cities

0   100   200 miles
0   100   200   300 km

Return to Tibet

PREFACE

My book *Seven Years in Tibet*, published in 1952 and soon translated into all major languages to become a worldwide success, possessed all the necessary ingredients for arousing exceptional interest. Like a well-crafted novel, it opened with an escape and ended with an escape; in between it provided an insight into the life of a country that very few strangers had been fortunate enough to see or experience.

Although the present book continues my personal experience of and in Tibet, the two books do not bear comparison with one another, any more than the external circumstances of my encounters with Tibet then and now can stand comparison. The journey which took me back in 1982 to the country that had molded my life was no longer an adventure: After many years of efforts to obtain an entry permit, efforts time and again coming up against a "not yet," I finally joined a tourist party as Tibet has recently been opened to a limited number of visitors each year.

As was to be expected, a number of books very rapidly appeared on the market, all of them marked by the fascination of Tibet. What

I hope will distinguish this book from all that has since been reported on Tibet is the juxtaposition of past and present, something that, apart from Hugh E. Richardson and A. R. Ford, I am the only one left in a position to provide. In consequence, my impressions are naturally different, always looking back, always related to the Tibet I used to know. I trust I shall be forgiven for regarding the Chinese-staged "thaw" with some skepticism: the words "it's all *dʒüma*"— "it's all eyewash"—muttered to me by my friends in Lhasa, still ring in my ears.

I cannot assume that all readers, especially the younger ones, are familiar with *Seven Years in Tibet,* published thirty years ago; but as acquaintance with many aspects and incidents is necessary to an understanding of my comparisons and accounts, I have inevitably had to repeat a number of things I wrote at that earlier time.

My principal purpose in writing this book has been to show how many valuable cultural treasures have been lost and how important it is now to find a way to safeguard the individual character and homeland of a people who are fascinating in so many respects, a people whose destiny is very close to my heart.

HEINRICH HARRER
August 1983

Departure

and

Homecoming

My head was buzzing from all the reports I had read in books and newspapers over the years since the Chinese occupation of Tibet in 1951. But these accounts, ranging inevitably from historical fact to personal impressions, could do nothing to satisfy my searching mind, my feelings, or the stored-up memories of my seven years' stay in Tibet. At long last, after several unsuccessful attempts to get Chinese permission to enter Tibet, I was sitting in an aircraft bound for Lhasa. After years of "not yet," the spring of 1982 at last saw the fulfillment of what had possibly been my greatest wish—after exactly thirty years—to return once more to the country that had become my second home, the country whose fate I had shared so keenly. Small wonder that I was feeling more excited than on any other journey, or that my senses were more alert than usual. I intended to put my trust in my instinct during the days to come, to compare and also to acknowledge; I determined to rely on my own eyes and to try to judge the reality before me with the help of my knowledge and experience.

It was a three hours' flight from Chengdu to the landing strip in the Brahmaputra valley, right in the center of Tibet. We were flying over high icy peaks of 6,000 and 7,000 meters (20,000–23,000 feet) and over the Tibetan plateau, lightly dusted with snow and lying below us with the same mysterious whiteness and immensity that Peter Aufschnaiter and I had experienced throughout two years during our escape. Then, there had been no maps and no reports of the route we intended to follow. We had had to advance into the unknown, always remembering to maintain a northeasterly course. We had been hoping to meet some nomads who might tell us the safest route and the distance to Lhasa. Our plan seemed rather harebrained even to us, and the icy winter storms we encountered in the frontier region provided a foretaste of what was to come.

It was on December 2, 1945, that we had left the inhabited Brahmaputra valley in order to cross the lonely Trans-Himalaya range. In the pit of my stomach I had the same sensation as on setting out to climb the north face of the Eiger or upon first catching sight of Nanga Parbat. I was wondering if we were not insanely overrating our own strength, and I did not calm down until I went into action and the point of no return lay behind. Yet if we had then even vaguely suspected what lay ahead of us, we would very probably have turned tail: before us was *terra incognita,* unknown to any man, and even on sketch maps of the region our paths would lead through blank areas, those blank areas which now, thirty-seven years later, I was for the first time seeing below me. Then, as now, I felt that I was face-to-face with the greatest infinity on earth. Except that this time I was in the seat of a heated, comfortable aircraft. That time, Aufschnaiter and I were on foot, permanently between 5,000 and 6,000 meters (16,000–20,000 feet). Seen from the air, the landscape was covered by a thin layer of snow, and an icy wind was sweeping across it. There was no sign of life anywhere, but I felt reassured when I spotted some small cairns built by nomads. To me

4

they were like a bridge to the gods from the loneliness of the inhospitable land.

I tried to take some photos through the portholes of the white veins winding between the mountains, which were in fact frozen streams. I still remembered the torture that walking in our poor footwear had been on that earlier occasion. The snow cover did not bear well, and several times we broke through, together with our yak. It had been a laborious progress, full of uncertainty about even the next few hours.

The gradual descent of the aircraft indicated that we were approaching Lhasa. My excitement rose as we flew east to west over the Brahmaputra valley; down there on the plateau must be Samye. The building had been erected by Padmasambhava in about A.D. 775, and it became the first communal settlement of Buddhist monks. Peter Aufschnaiter and I had made two excursions to the venerable monastery and I well remembered a conversation with the young Dalai Lama about the Tibetans' ancient wisdom about the separation of the body from the mind. Tibetan history records many saints who have been able to direct their minds to act hundreds of miles away, while their bodies were sitting immersed in deep meditation. The then sixteen-year-old Dalai Lama had been convinced that, thanks to his faith and with the aid of the prescribed rites, he too would learn to produce such effects over long distances.

He had wanted to send me to Samye and to direct me telepathically from Lhasa. I remember saying to him: "Well, Kundün, if you can do that I'll become a Buddhist myself!" Unfortunately the experiment was not staged, for the shadows of political catastrophe were already gathering. But that conversation has remained linked in my mind with the monastery of Samye.

What I now saw from the plane was a shock, although of course I had long known about it from reports—there were only ruins left of Samye; the entire monastery had been razed to the ground. As I now squeezed the trigger of my camera I remembered the many pictures I had taken of this religious center nearly forty years ago, pictures now sadly of only documentary value.

We were gliding over the Brahmaputra, which carried hardly any water in spring, and I recognized the first villages. Surely one should now see prayer flags waving in the wind and smell the smoke of yak-dung fires, I was thinking as I got off the plane. But instead there were Chinese meeting us in their plain and simple uniforms. And there, amidst that military monotony, suddenly a face: shy, friendly, familiar, Tibetan. It was Drölma, now forty-five, the wife of my old friend, Wangdü Sholkhang Tsetrung. Hesitantly we moved toward each other. She would not have been able to recognize me by sight: she had been a well-guarded child when I was also living at the Tsarong house. Although of course she knew my name and she knew about my arrival, she could know nothing of my thoughts. She gazed at me gravely, and a young woman ophthalmologist, who was traveling with me, later told me that these were the most beautiful and the saddest eyes she had ever seen.

I softly asked the reserved Tibetan woman if I might still call her Drölma as in the old days or if I had to address her now as Mrs. Sholkhang. "No, no, to you I am still the old Drölma," she said swiftly, but I felt it was no longer the same as before. While we were conversing in Tibetan, now a little more relaxed, our courier, a so-called National Guide from Peking, came up and snapped at me that if I needed anything I should ask him. I scarcely listened to him; I just looked at Drölma and thought about her background, her life and her fate. I was looking for the graceful movements, the cheerfulness and the carefree ease that had been typical features of young Tibetan women; but all I saw was seriousness and resignation.

Drölma was a daughter of the well-known Tsarong who had married three sisters. One of these was to become Rinchen Drölma

Taring, the author of the famous book *A Daughter of Tibet*, published in England by John Murray. Another of his wives was Drölma's mother. The third was Tsarong Pema Dolkar, whom I had known well in Lhasa and with whom he lived until his death.

The great Tsarong. They are enormously complicated, the family relationships of Tibetan nobles, permitting marriage to sisters-in-law and abounding in adoptions, so that a father might become an uncle overnight, or a niece a stepdaughter. The first great name in the dynasty was Tsarong Wangchuk Gyalpo; he was born in 1866, fathered ten children, and was assassinated at the behest of a jealous co-regent in Lhasa in 1912. He is known as Tsarong I, and he made a lot of enemies because he wanted to put an end to Tibet's isolation from the rest of the world. He introduced a number of things which until then had been unknown in Lhasa, such as the sewing machine, the camera, cigarettes and sweet tea.

Tsarong II, the second major figure of the dynasty, was not a child of Tsarong I but the son of an arrow maker who adopted the name of Tsarong. His real name was Chensal Namgang; he was a favorite of the Thirteenth Dalai Lama and was to become an even more important man than his father-in-law, Tsarong I. Admittedly he created some confusion in the family tree of the family he married into: first he married the second daughter of Tsarong I, then the fourth, and eventually the sixth—i.e., three sisters in succession. The son of his marriage with Pema Dolkar was Dadul Namgyal, who became Tsarong III, and, for his part, was the father of a Rinpoche, the name for any reincarnation.

Tsarong II was a superb administrator, even by Western standards, an outstanding diplomat who dared to oppose the Dalai Lama, a man forever trying to achieve reforms in his country, and a man whose wise counsel was sought on all important government matters. He was a self-made man in the most modern mold, and his abilities would have made him an outstanding personality in any

Western country. I shall never forget the gratitude I owe to Tsarong for having opened his house to Aufschnaiter and me, and for helping us to settle in Lhasa.

After 1956, when many nobles accompanied the Dalai Lama to Kalimpong, east of Darjeeling, in order to celebrate the 2,500th anniversary of the manifestation of Buddha, Tsarong remained in India. He and his family were not the only ones to seize that favorable opportunity: many wealthy Tibetans did not return to Lhasa. But whereas the others succeeded in making a new home for themselves in India, old Tsarong could not forget his native land. In 1958, in spite of warnings from his family and his friends, he decided to return to Tibet, in accordance with the view of many courageous Tibetans: "What you don't like in your country you must fight from within your country." Moreover, he was convinced from experience that he would soon get on good terms with the "foreigners" who had occupied his country, just as he had always been on good terms with all other foreigners who had visited Tibet.

When Tsarong returned to Lhasa, he had a conversation with Pala, the Chief Chamberlain of the Dalai Lama, who urged him to convince the Dalai Lama that he should not remain in Tibet. Pala said to him: "You are an experienced old man, you should talk to the Dalai Lama about it." Tsarong apparently had two conversations with the Dalai Lama. Thus, when Tibet was attacked by the Chinese in March 1959, the flight had all been arranged. The Tsongdü, the National Assembly, in continuous day-and-night session in the Potala, the palace-fortress of the Dalai Lama, with Tsarong present, demanded that, as an experienced Tibetan government official, he should stay behind in Lhasa. A few days later the Norbulingka, the garden in which the Dalai Lama's summer palace stands, was shelled, and Tsarong II was taken prisoner by the Chinese.

I managed to copy a frame from a Chinese film which showed three nobles being marched past the Chinese as prisoners, with hands raised high. One of these was Tsarong II. I held the picture in my hands for a long time, trying to fathom from the familiar features what he might be thinking at that time. I saw gravity and calm, yet also derision and contempt in the eyes of an idealist almost despairing of the fate of his nation, a man who could not reconcile himself to the fact that Tibet was not being given a chance to settle its own affairs. To him, justice ranked higher than any other virtue—and it was just this that was being denied to his people. He was one of those progressive men who knew full well that the aristocracy and monastic hierarchy would have to change in order to adjust Tibet's future destiny to the changed conditions of the world, and he endorsed the dictum of Garibaldi, which I once quoted to him: "If we want to remain as we are, certain things must be changed."

For him, the old hero, there was no future. On the morning of May 14, 1959, the day he was to have faced a great People's Court, to be humiliated by his own servants, he was found dead on his mattress in his prison cell. Perhaps he had taken his own life by swallowing some diamond splinters which—as he had once told me—he always carried secreted about his person. Death spared him the worst humiliation and injustice, a public trial by a People's Court.

On my second arrival in Lhasa it was spring in Tibet and the sun was brilliantly bright. I took photographs, and recalled that, in 1952, when I got back to Europe with my few slides, no one would believe the colors—the film, everyone said, must be faulty and the colors were not true: no sky could be that blue, no water could sparkle that green. But now, thirty years later, we once more beheld these incredibly intense colors, that hard azure-blue, that eye-calming green of the grass on the very first day on the banks of the Kyichu, a tributary of the Brahmaputra. Of course, the altitude is a major factor in these colors, and the dust-free air at 4,000 meters (13,000 feet) makes them emerge with a special intensity and purity.

2

LHASA
THEN AND
NOW

We drove into Lhasa by bus, and I confess that I felt some trepidation about how I would react to the city.

The first temple we were shown along the road, immediately upon arrival, was well preserved. About twenty miles south of Lhasa, at Nethang, was the Drölmalhakhang temple; although the small chapel nearby with the principal relic-tomb of Atisha, the great religious reformer, had been destroyed, another *chöten* enshrining some of his relics had been miraculously preserved. This was almost certainly due to its remote position, or it may have been one of those monuments which Chou En-lai, the Chinese Foreign Minister, was said to have given personal orders to protect. We admired the beautiful frescoes, were impressed by the four guardians—huge clay figures—and were made welcome by a friendly temple employee who most willingly showed us everything and was delighted to hear me speak Tibetan. Not until later, when I had seen all the destruction in the country, did I fully appreciate the good fortune that had preserved this temple and the fact that we were allowed to roam about it freely and take photographs without having to pay, and were in fact almost pampered.

After this we were taken to the government "Guest House," where we would be accommodated for the entire duration of our stay, constantly "looked after" by the two National Guides. Initially there was some degree of nervousness between them and us, and although we did not exactly make friends with them, we subsequently got used to each other. Provided I went about it the right way, I even had some of my requests complied with. One of these was a meeting with my old friend Wangdü, the husband of Drölma, with whom I desperately wanted to have a talk. I had heard and read too many controversial stories about him and his attitude; I wanted to question him myself. My application, which I had to address officially to the Tourist Bureau in Lhasa, at first remained unanswered.

Before I could let Wangdü know that I was in Lhasa—he had been thirty when I last saw him—I had another unexpected encounter at the Guest House. On my very first day, in the late afternoon, a handsome Tibetan approached me and said: "Don't you recognize me, Henrig?" I stammered a little and remarked that, after all, thirty years had passed and he would have to help me a little. "But you saved my life, don't you remember that?" he replied. Of course, now I remembered. He was Jigme, the son of Surkhang, Tibet's secular Foreign Minister, the first person that Aufschnaiter and I had called on. One day I had been the guest of Foreign Minister Surkhang and his family, who had pitched a tent on the riverbank. The only son of his second marriage, Jigme—which means "fear naught"—was home on vacation. He was attending school in India and had learned to swim a little. I was in the water, floating on my back, and had drifted some way downstream when I suddenly heard screaming and saw a wildly gesticulating crowd on the bank, pointing to the river. Something must have happened. I quickly swam to the bank and ran back to the campground. Just then Jigme's body bobbed up in a vortex, was dragged down again, emerged once more . . . Without reflecting I dived into the water. I too was caught by the undercurrent, but I was stronger than young Jigme and managed to bring his lifeless body to the bank. My experience as a sports teacher stood me in good stead, and after a short while the boy was breathing again—to the joy of his father and the amazed spectators. With tears in his eyes, the Foreign Minister assured me time and again that he was well aware that but for me his son would have drowned.

And now this son stood before me, a few decades later, as large as life. He had spent twenty years in prison and concentration camps, but the political thaw had recently enabled him to make a livelihood for himself as a trekking official. This may sound rather grand but was in fact a job without any responsibility or independence. One of the Chinese supervised everything he did.

It was evening in Lhasa and my fellow travelers had gone to bed. Most of them were suffering from the altitude; after all, we had come up from 400 to 3,600 meters (1,300 to 12,000 feet) in three hours. They deserved their rest, but I could not possibly think of sleep. I was far too excited during these first few hours. I stood outside the entrance to the Guest House and drank in the night; I felt the vast landscape around Lhasa throbbing with a mysterious life. Why, I reflected, was I so sad, now that at last I had arrived in Lhasa, the object of my longing? I felt no tiredness; on the contrary, I was in a strange state of superawakeness. To miss the first night in Tibet by sleeping seemed unthinkable.

The next morning I walked about the grounds and discovered that we were surrounded by dozens of hutments for Chinese troops. I found an orchard plantation, and an old man working there remembered that, all those years ago, I had introduced the "marriage" of trees, as they called improvement by grafting, and he told me that they did things quite differently now under the Chinese. This was my third conversation with a Tibetan, after Drölma and Surkhang Jigme, and I felt similarly moved, especially in that setting. Over there stood the Potala, seemingly quite close to me, yet it would take about two hours' walk to reach it. To the right gleamed the roofs of the Norbulingka, with the outlines of the Kyichu valley beyond it. Behind the Guest House was that mountain which, in the old days, the Dalai Lama would visit once a year, riding to the top on a white yak. A hermitage, harmoniously built into the steep slope, had disappeared. Doubts, normally unknown to me, overcame me: was I really where I had hoped to be . . . ?

A few days later we visited the Potala and inspected the monasteries. In every temple we needed to have quite a few *yüan* ready if we wanted to take pictures. Those in power had developed a system of calculating the charges for taking photographs. In one monastery, for instance, there was a flat charge of 100 *yüan*—about $50—while elsewhere one might be charged 10 *yüan* ($5) per altar or per snapshot, so that in a large and interesting temple one could easily spend $100 if one wanted to take pictures of everything of interest.

This did not mean, however, that one also purchased the right to choose what to photograph. Everywhere we were watched, spied on, followed and observed, to make sure no prohibited pictures were taken. Once, when one of us took a secret photograph without permission, we were all made to leave our cameras outside the temple for the duration of the sightseeing; of course, there was protest and a lot of difficulties. Each day we received fresh instructions from the Chinese tour leaders and from our interpreter on what was permitted and what was forbidden. These things gave rise to irritation and annoyance, but there was also some amusement—we once saw the inscription: "Taking photographs here is prohibited free of charge."

However, it was not just the Chinese who acted so rigidly. In the Norbulingka, the former summer residence of the Dalai Lama, it was a young Tibetan woman, Mingma, who, with her hard features and her hair severely tied back in a ponytail, in an attempt to out-Chinese the Chinese, enforced the ban on photography in an almost intolerable manner. When I spoke to her in Tibetan and observed that surely these were all new paintings, she haughtily ignored me. The Chinese put forward a dubious argument for these strict rules: to date they had not published the frescoes, and until Chinese scholars had researched them thoroughly no one else was allowed to do so. I did not bother to tell them that these very frescoes in the Norbulingka had been commissioned in 1954 by Jigme Taring, a cabinet minister now living in exile, and Thupten W. Pala, the Chief Chamberlain, when the Dalai Lama returned to India and a new palace had just been built for him in the summer garden. These two men were well acquainted with the historical writings and knew what motifs should be painted. There was, therefore, nothing there to conceal—but the Chinese probably did not know that. I could have gone straight to Dehra-Dun to find out from Jigme what scenes he had commissioned, or to Amdo Jampa, the artist, whom I had known well.

Nevertheless, I was disappointed not to be allowed to photograph the frescoes in the Dalai Lama's principal throne room, for there is one picture whose subject is of particular interest to me: in the upper half of the painting, the Dalai Lama is enthroned, surrounded by all his relatives and officials. These were the very people who had been my friends or my superiors in Lhasa. I knew them all—the Dalai Lama's mother and father, the ministers, the Kalön Lama, Lobsang Samten and the ambassadors. Until 1981 there had been no ban on taking photographs of these frescoes, so enough pictures of them exist. They are in fact somewhat tasteless, since the artist had copied the heads from photographs and subsequently colored them, but even so they are of great documentary value. I stood for a long time gazing at the individual faces of people who, for several years, had been dear friends of mine.

The arbitrary manner in which the ban on photography is practiced by the Chinese is illustrated by an experience we had at the
Tashilhünpo monastery, where several hundred monks are once
more living. It contains the famous Ngagpa-Dratsang, a college of
the monastic university, where some thirty scholars—men with
twenty or thirty years of study behind them—perform their divine
rites. There, taking photographs is totally forbidden. I am all in
favor of men who meditate not being disturbed, but it was only
photography that was forbidden there—not entry to the meditation
rooms. In consequence, tourists were scuttling about between the
rows of lamas, peering over their shoulders into their books and,
with no inhibitions, inspecting the altar. In my opinion this should
have been prohibited too; Tibetan monks should be given the quiet
they need. Incidentally, this was the only time we saw monks at
prayer; admittedly they were so old and their habits so tattered and
dirty that I thought this might be the reason why they did not let
us take pictures. No charge was made for wandering about the
monastery.

HOW
IT ALL STARTED

It was on January 15, 1946, that Peter Aufschnaiter and I, after being on the run for nearly two years, descended from the Changthang, the northerly highlands, and, from the wide Kyichu valley, first caught sight of the golden roofs of the Potala gleaming in the distance. This spot—called Kyentsal Lupding, ten kilometers (six miles) from Lhasa—was one that I was to revisit frequently during the next few years. I called it "the place of parting and reunion," because it was one of the many attractive customs of the Tibetans that friends setting out on a pilgrimage, or nobles leaving for India, or children returning from boarding school, were seen off and welcomed at this spot. Tents were put up, small folding tables were laid, and everybody joined in a happy picnic. A place of welcome and parting, therefore, to which travelers were frequently accompanied by a large column on horseback, where tea was drunk and *khata*, white silk good-luck scarves, were exchanged. I loved these ceremonies and wanted to see the place again.

If I had not seen the magnificent Potala in the distance, towering above everything, I would never have recognized the old spot: before me extended one huge gray industrial zone with ugly buildings, a dusty cement factory, gravel works and concrete roads. The reality of 1982. I had before me now the drab picture of a country once characterized by religion, where monasteries had been encountered at every step, and where rock faces had yard-high figures of deities carved into them, painted in brilliant natural colors. There had been the prayer walls too with their *Om-mani-padme-hum* stones. Even then, of course, one used to come across the ruins of ancient fortresses which had been destroyed in the Muslim assault, or old farmsteads which had been abandoned through lack of water for the fields—but those were the kind of ruins which resulted from the passage of time all over the world and which therefore did not arouse the same sadness as did this modern destruction caused by political hatred and fanaticism.

The same ceremonies of welcome and farewell were practiced also on the dam which we ourselves had built thirty years ago against the floods of the Kyichu. From there many travelers from Lhasa would go by yak-hide boat to the spot where the Kyichu flowed into the Brahmaputra. This voyage, in comfort, took them seven or eight hours, compared with the two days it would take them on horseback. The animals with their loads would be sent ahead with the servants; then everybody would meet again at the small settlement of Chu-Shü, cross the river by wooden ferry and continue on horseback toward the Himalayas.

This dam had been built by Aufschnaiter and myself in the spring of 1948; it needed to be completed in time for the monsoon, so that the floods should not, as used to be an annual occurrence, threaten the summer palace. Each of the many workers we employed was paid his wages every day. This produced continual good humor, and the work prospered. There was great confusion each time they dug up a worm. They would carefully place it on a shovel and carry it away a good distance to save its life. Respect for all creatures is very marked among Buddhists, and no one would ever harm an animal.

Naturally, on this visit to Tibet I went out to the dam to see if it still stood. Indeed, it had withstood the floods over all these years and, because it was so good and wide, Russian-made jeeps were driving over it past me along the river. It was afternoon as I sat on the edge of the dam, thinking back to the old days. Typical of spring, and indeed a characteristic of that season, are the sudden and literally blinding sandstorms. The sand grits between one's teeth and penetrates one's clothes and shoes. The Chinese had supplied us with the familiar mouth masks one sees in all the pictures, and some of us actually wore them. Along with the sandstorms comes the first delicate verdure on the willows, young shoots appear everywhere, and everyone rejoices that winter is over. The first tree to display that golden-green haze was *Jo Utra*, "Buddha's hair," a huge twin-trunked willow which used to stand outside the main entrance to the Tsuglagkhang, its enormous branches shading everything—the smallpox pillar, the Doring and the whole square. But vandals had wrecked that most beautiful of all trees, from which no pious Tibetan would have ever broken a twig. Only the naked trunk of this living shrine now towered into the skies, interpreted by the Tibetans as Buddha's warning finger.

Back in 1946, as we approached Lhasa, we had covered the last few miles with a stream of pilgrims and caravans. Soon we recognized the features of the city we had so often admired in books—the Chagpori, the hill on which stood one of two medical schools, and Drepung, the world's largest monastery, where 10,000 monks were living. It was a veritable town, with many stone buildings and hundreds of gilded spires surmounting the roofs. A little below were the terraces of the Nechung monastery which for hundreds of years had housed Tibet's greatest mystery, the state oracle questioned on all major government decisions. More and more clearly the outlines of the Potala had emerged, and finally we had reached the Western Gate of the city of Lhasa.

Until 1949 we led a peaceful and happy life in the capital and its magnificent surroundings, when suddenly news came of Chinese mounted regiments and infantry concentrating in the east of the country, along the frontier. Nationalist China had never reconciled itself to the loss of Tibet and Outer Mongolia; but now it was the political opponents of Chiang Kai-shek who, during the months and years to follow, made every effort to incorporate Tibet.

On October 7, 1950, Mao's troops advanced into the interior of the country. The first clashes occurred at six points along the frontier. We in Lhasa were still hoping for a miracle. But the Chinese penetrated deeper into the country and so the National Assembly in Lhasa addressed an appeal to the United Nations, asking for help against the aggressors. But at that time no one was interested in Tibet. The UN merely expressed its hope that China and Tibet would come to some peaceful compromise ...

It then became clear to everybody that Tibet must surrender to its superior enemy. All those who did not wish to live under Chinese rule began to pack their belongings. Aufschnaiter and I realized that the time had come when we must leave our second homeland. The thought greatly depressed us.

One disastrous report followed another. The question of the young Dalai Lama's fate now arose. However, this was too grave a decision to be taken by the government alone: the advice of the gods had to be asked. In the presence of the Dalai Lama and the Regent two balls of barley flour were kneaded, their weights being tested on golden scales until they were exactly the same. Two slips of paper bearing the words Yes and No were rolled into balls and these were thrown into a golden beaker. The beaker was pressed into the hands of the state oracle, who was already performing his trancelike dance.

He spun the vessel faster and faster, until at last one ball leaped out and fell to the ground. It contained the Yes, and so it was decided that the Dalai Lama must leave Lhasa.

I myself set off in mid-November 1950, making my way to the south, with a detour, that same month, from Gyangtse to Shigatse, Tibet's second-largest city, famous for its monastery of Tashilhünpo, the seat of the Panchen Lama. He is a high incarnation, played off by the Chinese for many generations against the Dalai Lama. The present Panchen Lama had been educated in China; he was then proclaimed by those in power to be the rightful ruler and entered Tibet, for the first time, with the Chinese troops. I shall deal with this tragic and courageous figure in a later chapter.

The Chinese had halted their advance and kept inviting the Lhasa government to send envoys to Peking for negotiations. On May 23, 1951, a Tibetan delegation headed by Kalön Ngabö Ngawang Jigme—still the most important collaborator and the commander of the Tibetan troops in Kham who had weakly surrendered to the Chinese—signed a seventeen-point agreement which stripped the Tibetans of the right to independent foreign policy and defense decisions but otherwise left them their internal autonomy.

Ngabö Ngawang Jigme, of all people—an illegitimate child adopted by nobles and now the most famous "two-headed" one, as collaborators are known in Tibet. In my Lhasa days he used to play mah-jongg day and night, and for very high stakes at that. Mah-jongg is a game not unlike dominoes. Previously it was extremely popular and was played passionately; nowadays scarcely a mah-jongg player can be found in Tibet: only once, in the courtyard of the Dalai Lama's house, now a hotel for Tibetan minorities, did I see a few people playing for very low stakes. What has remained is Sho, a dice game: the dice are placed in a wooden bowl which is shaken and tipped out onto a leather board. Beans and cowrie shells are used for chips.

Ngabö wrote the preface to one of the first books on Tibet, produced by a team of Chinese authors under the plain title of *Tibet*. I can only assume that he never read the book, or that perhaps his name was put under a preface written for him by the Chinese. Surely he must know, better than most, that the statement on page 117 is nonsense and a lie: "At one time the troupes of actors performed only for the Dalai Lama at the Norbulingka, the summer palace in Lhasa, whereas today the performances are open to the public." I myself witnessed, and indeed photographed and filmed, thousands of Tibetans attending these festivities at the Norbulingka every year. They were not allowed inside the yellow wall which enclosed the Dalai Lama's private garden, but that was not where the performances were held. They were held, then as now, within the great wall that runs around the Norbulingka. And this, I repeat, was accessible to the people. Thus, even Ngabö participates in that *dzüma*, the Tibetan term for a deception.

To do them justice, one should not conceal some positive aspects of the activity of collaborators. Tibetans told me that some time previously Ngabö made a trip to Lhasa from Peking, where he now lives as Tibet's representative, and requested to be shown a Lhasa school. On discovering that all the pupils were Chinese, he used his influence to ensure that Tibetan children could attend that school as well. It is to be hoped that, even in the minds of collaborators, love of Tibet and a sense of belonging to the Tibetan people have not entirely vanished.

To return to history. The Dalai Lama fled Lhasa at that time; however, when he reached the Indian frontier in the Chumbi valley in southern Tibet, he hesitated at first about leaving his country. I myself stayed with him until March 1951, when I decided to leave Tibet. I knew I could not return to Lhasa, but I was still employed by the Tibetan government and, at least formally, had to apply to be granted leave of absence. Permission was given at once. I received a passport valid for six months, with an endorsement requesting the Indian government to assist me with my return. It was a sad parting and I was worried about the fate of the young Lama ruler and his country. Mao Tse-tung's overpowering shadow lay menacingly over Tibet. In the summer of the same year the Dalai Lama returned to Lhasa. I witnessed the Chinese governor-general of Tibet passing through India to assume his rule in Lhasa. And on September 9, 1951, the first contingent of the "people's liberation" army entered the capital. Before long, the whole of Tibet was occupied by Chinese troops.

Initially, the soldiers were disciplined and correct, but when the army grew to 250,000, the burden it represented was such that the country suffered, and only the will of the occupying power, which was settling down comfortably in Lhasa, counted for anything. Peasants were compelled to make their modest means of transport available for road building, and their beasts of burden were employed so ruthlessly that many of them died. But as early as 1954 the Chinese proudly pointed to the first graveled road linking Lhasa with Szechwan province, a road whose sole purpose was to bind the subjected country even more firmly to China and to facilitate further troop convoys to Tibet. To the Tibetans it was of no use whatever. The forced "voluntary" employment on the construction of an airport, allegedly to serve the economic development of the country, likewise supported China's expansionist aspirations. Contrary to Chinese reports, the Tibetans' standard of living had greatly declined. Foodstuffs had become so expensive that hardly anyone could afford the prices, and, for the first time in Tibetan history, there was genuine famine.

The Tibetans could not accept these conditions and therefore composed a six-point note of protest, in which they described their living conditions and demanded improvements. The response of the Red rulers was a ban on all criticism of communism. The Chinese, on the other hand, interfered in everything, from the administration of the monasteries to the directives of the aristocratic ruling class, though surprisingly they treated the nobility far better than the people. The Dalai Lama and progressive nobles had, of course, long realized that reforms were indispensable, for instance, for correcting the unjust distribution of cultivable land, one-third of which belonged to monasteries, nobles or government officials. I know from numerous conversations that the Dalai Lama fully realized his country's backwardness; there exists a plan of reforms produced by him in 1954, a sensible plan that would have been beneficial to the people. It may seem to run counter to common sense—but the Chinese prevented the Tibetans from introducing their own reforms. They looted the monasteries, and drove out the lamas or put them under arrest. This vandalism was too much for the Tibetans. Once again it was the brave and intelligent Khampas who, from their province of Kham, vigorously resisted oppression by a foreign power.

Colonialism, of course, came to an end after the Second World War, but I find that a kind of neocolonialism or "liberation colonialism" has replaced the old empires throughout the world. This is true also in Tibet. The Tibetans, after all, have their own language, writing and religion. Their customs and traditions, their hairstyles and their clothes are all totally different from the Chinese. And yet the Chinese regard them as belonging to them. But the Tibetans want their own autonomous state, comparable perhaps to the position of Mongolia vis-à-vis the Soviet Union, and they have the legitimate hope that all Tibetans, including those in Amdo and eastern Kham, will be included in a united Tibet.

How little this situation or the geographical conditions are understood in Peking, and how far the Chinese people themselves are from regarding Tibet as a part of China, is shown by an experience I had during a subsequent stay in Peking. At the reception desk in my hotel I asked a Chinese girl for postage stamps for one letter abroad and two to friends of mine in Lhasa. Unhesitatingly, she stuck the same stamps on all three. I asked: "Isn't that too much? Surely Tibet isn't abroad?" She looked surprised, disappeared, and had to have a colleague explain to her that Tibet was a part of China. In spite of an undoubtedly good political schooling, the Chinese girl at the hotel had clearly never heard of it.

After this experience I tested the girl clerk at my next hotel, with the same result: again she did not know that Tibet was regarded as a part of China. It should be remembered that these hotel employees are relatively educated people, speak a foreign language and deal with hundreds of foreigners. That they are unaware of Tibet's occupation is certainly most surprising. But I have noticed before, to my surprise, that we in the West are better informed on events in Tibet than the average Chinese.

But back to Lhasa. The revolt in the eastern Tibetan province of Kham was to go on for fifteen years; for two years it also spread to Amdo in the north. Then began a period of unimaginable atrocities by the Chinese. I do not wish to write about all those murders and barbaric tortures; that has been done often enough and the evidence is readily available. One man's destiny only, typical of many, will be the subject of a later chapter: an account which the Dalai Lama's physician recorded for me on tape.

When I left the Chumbi valley for India in 1951, I was still hoping that the seventeen-point agreement between Tibet and China might make for possible coexistence between two such unequal partners. But my hopes were dashed. Neither the Dalai Lama's willingness to meet the conditions of the treaty nor the Tibetans' moderation succeeded in ensuring their promised independence. The Chinese probably never intended to keep to the agreement; on the contrary, there was oppression and cruelty. The "road to socialism" prescribed by the Chinese called for a complete transformation of the Tibetan way of life. However, throughout thirty years of occupation, efforts to shake their religious beliefs have proved a total failure—and it was this which seems to have been a major objective of the Chinese. Once they had exterminated their faith, total annexation would be an easy step. However, the Tibetans are clinging to their religion more than ever, since that alone provides support and consolation to them in these difficult times. The pillage and destruction of ancient monasteries and of irreplaceable cultural treasures has been a tragedy for the Tibetans and for the entire world—but they have merely strengthened the defiant resistance of an oppressed people.

By now the whole world knows how, under the rule of the "Gang of Four," the people were deprived of the economic basis of their existence and monks were pressed into forced labor and into abandoning their celibacy. Many of the best spiritual leaders and teachers were executed. And, while thousands of Tibetans were forcibly resettled in China, thousands of Chinese settlers arrived in Tibet. It was hoped to make the Tibetans a minority in their own country. The process of transformation was to be accomplished by a reeducation of young Tibetans and by other "socialist measures." The result was covert and overt resistance by the population.

The next steps taken by the Chinese were land reforms. Attempts were made to incite the peasants against their masters, and these attempts were successful with some malcontents. But many of the feudal landlords were Khampas, an exceptionally tough and upright people who would not accept such treatment without opposition. It is not therefore surprising that it was from their ranks that there came a hero and liberator of the Tibetan people. He was twenty-four-year-old Andrugtshang, the head of one of the oldest, richest and most esteemed families in Kham. Andrugtshang was known throughout Tibet as a benign, helpful man, always one of the first to put his hand in his pocket when others were in need. This man now took to the woods and became the leader of a group of Tibetan friends whose aim was to fight the Chinese. The Khampa partisans succeeded in gaining control over a considerable area, to the extent that the Chinese soldiers hardly ventured out of their barracks. In the autumn of 1958 the Khampas felt strong enough to risk open battle. The engagement near Tsethang, a market town south of the Brahmaputra, lasted several hours and several thousand Chinese were killed. This was the greatest victory of the brave Khampas.

The Tibetans are a peaceful people. They never raise their voices when a soft answer might prevent a quarrel. Now, when the Chinese asked the Dalai Lama to send his bodyguards into battle against the seemingly invincible Khampas, he replied courteously that he would be pleased to do so but his soldiers were too ill-equipped and besides would probably go over to the Khampas.

In the spring of 1959 another popular rising broke out in Lhasa. The occasion was an invitation to the Dalai Lama to attend a theatrical performance at the Chinese headquarters in Lhasa. The invitation was suspected—probably with justification—of being a cover for an intended abduction. A protective wall of people surrounded the summer palace of the young king; 30,000 Tibetans were prepared to defend their spiritual and secular leader with their own bodies. In the end it was one of those much-dreaded sandstorms which on March 17 enabled the Dalai Lama, his family, his teachers, ministers and a retinue of eighty companions, guards and servants to escape from the Norbulingka unobserved. They made their way southward into Khampa-controlled territory and across the border into India.

The Chinese did not discover the flight until March 20. Even the Tibetans surrounding the palace thought the Dalai Lama and his court were still inside, and so they looked on in horror when, on March 19, the Chinese began systematically destroying the palace compound from the outside in, a few yards at a time. Many Tibetans lost their lives resisting this (as they saw it) murderous action; and their resistance prevented the Chinese from guessing the truth. When the escape became known there ensued a bloody two-day war in Lhasa, during which 800 more Tibetans lost their lives and many houses and temples were bombed. Strikingly, one of the leaders of the Tibetan side was Ngawang Sengi, a businessman's son whom the Chinese had considered particularly promising and had educated in Peking for a position in the new regime.

Before the guns fell silent, thousands more Tibetans died; and, as a final measure of repression, the Chinese arrested all surviving males in Lhasa between the ages of sixteen and sixty and deported them to China as forced laborers.

On March 31, 1959, the Dalai Lama reached the Indian border, where he and his party were protected by the Indian army. The Chinese claimed that the uprising in Tibet had been the work of "reactionary classes," but many of those who eventually fled to India were simple folk; and, as early as January 1959, the army of resistance had committed itself in writing to a broad program of social and political reform.

THE LURE OF
TIBET

An enormous amount has been reported about Tibet in the past and a lot is still being written about that country. I like to call it the "lure of Tibet," that fascination and attraction of a mysterious realm which for centuries has fired man's imagination and spirit of adventure. The most informative, of course, are the books written by explorers like Sven Hedin and Wilhelm Filchner, whose work was mainly geographical. Nowadays there are a number of Tibetologists who write on Tibet, not for commercial reasons but out of love of the country and, of course, from scientific interest. Most of these went to the trouble of learning the Tibetan language. I cannot enumerate them all; I will name but three of the many: Siegbert Hummel, Blanche Ch. Olshak and David L. Snellgrove, whose books and scholarly studies have passed on to us their vast knowledge of Tibetan culture. They based themselves on the fundamental work of Charles Bell and Hugh E. Richardson, who spent many years in Tibet and wrote from personal experience about Tibetan customs, way of life and art. Much read, though less scholarly, are the books by Alexandra David-Neel who, because of her love of Tibetan culture and religion, became a Buddhist nun and who was convinced of the existence of the supernatural, including the separation of mind and body, levitation and mysticism.

In view of the fact that, until a few years ago, descriptions of Tibetan life and religious myths were exceedingly difficult if not impossible to verify, since hardly anybody was able to visit the country, it is not surprising that there were also authors who cheerfully wrote down whatever their imagination prompted. I myself was involved in the unmasking of one such case. During a lecture tour in England, my publisher Rupert Hart-Davis told me that there was a sensational new book about Tibet. His friend, Frederick Warburg, the publisher of the book, sent the galleys for us to see. I glanced through the text and immediately realized that the author was a fraud. It was a book by Lobsang Rampa, who claimed to have worked in Lhasa as a student and physician for many years at the time that I had been there; it was called *The Third Eye*. I asked Hart-Davis to phone Frederick Warburg and ask if I could not meet Lobsang Rampa as it would be interesting for me to speak Tibetan to somebody who had lived in Lhasa at the same time as me. But all I got was excuses: he was meditating and could not talk to me; a few days later I was told that he was terribly sorry but he was on his way to Canada. It was becoming increasingly clear to me that he was a fake; Hugh Richardson, the British representative in Lhasa when I was there, some other Tibetologists, and I now tried to unmask the man. Eventually Marco Pallis, a Tibetologist and devout Buddhist who played the cello in a group of chamber musicians and was an expert on Tibetan carpets, undertook to track him down. He hired a detective who pretended to be a disciple of Lobsang Rampa and discovered that, among others, members of the English nobility were visiting him for meditation. With a flowing beard and surrounded by Siamese cats, he sat on a huge bed—but he was in fact the son of a Devonshire plumber who had been in a car accident and, after a while, become a fortuneteller.

When he discovered that people would believe anything provided it was served up to them skillfully, Lobsang Rampa began to write books on Tibet and to enrich them with mysticism from other spiritual spheres. The result was *The Third Eye,* which sold millions of copies all over the world.

If somebody writes fiction, as James Hilton did in *Lost Horizon,* that, in my opinion, is entirely in order. But if somebody perjures himself by describing as documentation something that is pure invention, then this is something that should be stopped. Alexandra David-Neel, for instance, whenever she admits to having believed something as a Buddhist, invariably uses very cautious phrases prefaced by "I have been told . . ." She never says: "It was like that"— and this is the fundamental difference.

What I call "the lure of Tibet" is the special status which Tibet has always occupied in world opinion. Scarcely any other people have aroused so much concern. Take India, for example. When, after independence and partition, India had ten million refugees of its own, this seemed far less significant to the world than the 100,000 Tibetan exiles who enjoyed universal sympathy. So much were they the center of attention that Krishna Menon, India's representative in the UN, angrily leaped to his feet in a General Assembly and exclaimed: "Always Tibet! Always Tibet! Why?"

Why indeed? It was a mystical country, a nation hardly anybody knew. Its monasteries were large, mysterious and remote, hidden behind icy peaks. One could invest in it all one's dreams and longings. There were stories of monks who could fly through the air and who were able to separate their minds from their bodies. There were hardly any travelers to bring back tales from the country, and the few who had been there often could not resist the temptation to relate adventures which did not always correspond to the truth.

Now that the Chinese Communists, of all people, in their anxiety to earn hard currency, had suddenly opened the doors of Tibet, a

dozen picture books instantly appeared with beautiful color photographs but with texts often compiled from other, earlier books.
Frequently the sources were very old works, and the mistakes in
them were adopted. There is scarcely a single genuine documentary
account among them; moreover, most of the books are politically
biased. A typical example is Han Suyin, who, being a Communist,
found everything marvelous and who paid fulsome tribute to the
Chinese for their "positive transformations in Tibet." The outstanding example of the opposite extreme is the book by Peter-Hannes
Lehmann. He writes from the Tibetan point of view, mainly that of
the Dalai Lama's sister, Pema Gyalpo, who, like himself, had stood
speechless before the horrors and destruction a year after the end of
the cultural revolution. Since then, certain things have improved and
rather more toleration is being practiced—yet everything Lehmann
has described is in line with the facts, reveals his great knowledge
about Tibet, and is therefore of lasting value.

Certainly it is difficult to do justice to everyone—the Tibetan
refugees, the Tibetan collaborators, and people like Pema Gyalpo
who, with her great and understandable love of her compatriots,
finds it difficult, after the horrors she has experienced, to perceive
and to believe the few positive transformations. But one has to try
to do justice also to the Chinese, since there is now an undoubted
change for the better. They had a great opportunity, but unfortunately they failed to use it. I am reminded of a conversation I had
with a Tibetan minister in Lhasa in 1949. When I asked him which
way the Tibetans would incline supposing they had to join one of
the great powers—India, Russia or China—he answered me very
briefly: "Just look at me!" That was in Chiang Kai-shek's day, when
Tibetans naturally felt closer to the old China. Today, after all the
atrocities and frightful experiences, he would probably be less certain. The mistake the Chinese made was their failure to win friends.
Instead they made enemies of the Tibetans.

5

SHANGRI-LA,
A DREAM OF
MANKIND

During my short stay in Peking I was, like any other tourist, taken from one temple to another, from imperial tomb to sculpted deity. Some were still in ruins, others had been preserved, and much had been rebuilt. After all, it should not be forgotten that the "Gang of Four" had raged just as much at home as it had in Tibet, except—and this again confirms my "lure of Tibet" theory— that everyone knew about Tibet and very few knew about China at the time. In spite of the demystification of the temples through Chinese devastation they have not lost their fascination for me.

Peking's "Forbidden City," the holiest of holies of the kingdom and formerly cut off from profane eyes by a multitude of walls, is nowadays the meeting point of all tourists to China. It has become a typical tourist sight, and the Chinese are proud of it. It is something between art, applied art and imitation—just as the countless souvenir stalls piled high with kitsch are a symptom of the new adaptation to tourism. This was what Lhasa would be like one day, I thought, as I remembered the more than 1,000 tourists in 1981. Before long the souvenir trash would be on sale at the foot of the Potala. The first shy beginnings were already to be seen: little amulet cases made from cheap aluminum and set with false turquoise and corals, were already being offered as antiques to the inexperienced traveler on Barkhor, the ring road of ancient Lhasa. Manufacture of these trinkets might be somewhat restricted by a recent Chinese ruling that no more than 400 tourists per annum are to be allowed into Lhasa.

This, of course, is another problem: by what right can a living city be cut off from tourism, its gates opened to only a limited number of tourists, as though it were a private museum? Tibetans, too, want a share in the tourist bonanza, they want to make money like the rest of the world in order to raise their standard of living— whether this means improving it is debatable. For the present, all the gate moneys go to Peking.

The dubious nature of such "improvements" and the problems presented by tourism can be experienced in Ladakh. I am also thinking of the small neighboring kingdom of Zanskar with its 12,000 inhabitants. Maybe I was the last person to get there on horseback along rough tracks. Today a road leads into that country and it is accessible by bus. And what did the King of Zanskar say to me when I expressed regret that in future there would be dust and gasoline fumes instead of the sky and the fragrant flowers? "I want my subjects, too, to have a hospital and a post office, and that is made possible by tourism, and for that I need the road."

It is estimated that some 3,400 foreigners have visited Tibet since it opened its frontiers. If the number of visas is now to be restricted to 400 per year, it is easy to guess the reason: for years the Chinese have been telling the Tibetans that they would at last live in the communist paradise, where everyone was better off than anywhere else in the world. Now these wealthy tourists, well-dressed and equipped with photographic and film cameras, were proving the opposite. This is not the only reason for the cutback; organizational problems probably play a part too.

A Tibetan boy of thirteen told me that the children in Lhasa were told at school to keep away from tourists as far as possible and avoid contact with them. "But we don't," he said, "we always creep up to the strangers whenever they arrive in order to get close to them. They smell so good."

When Peter Aufschnaiter and I were living in Lhasa, Tibet was "the roof of the world." It had an aura of the unattainable, the unknown and the mystical. A dream mankind wanted to dream, complete with abominable snowman and mysterious Shangri-la. Was anything of this left in Tibet?

"Shangri-la" is a name from James Hilton's famous novel *Lost Horizon,* a book that was a huge success, was several times made into a film and is still selling after forty years. It starts with a plane making a forced landing somewhere in the Himalayas, near a monastery, and that spot Hilton called Shangri-la. It is instantly clear that the location must be in Tibet, since monks live there in prayer and with mysterious music. The term Shangri-la acquired especial fame through President Roosevelt in the Second World War. Asked by journalists about the whereabouts of a particular aircraft carrier, Roosevelt, to avoid disclosing whether it had been sunk or was still afloat at sea, said: "She's at Shangri-la." After the novel and the presidential remark the name became known worldwide; now there are hotels, restaurants and bars calling themselves Shangri-la, in the hope of suggesting mystery, the supernatural and unattainable beauty.

I was hoping during my stay in Lhasa that something of that magic had survived in Tibet, so that there should be one country left on earth where superstition would be the poetry of life, where there would be room for mysterious rites, where there would still be oracles, astrologers, miracle healers and mystics—not charlatans like Lobsang Rampa, but people with a genuine faith of the kind the Tibetans possess in such rich measure, the faith that truly moves mountains.

When speaking of Tibetan mysteries and miracles there is no need to invent stories; there are enough genuine "miracles" in this land. I am thinking, for instance, of the 6,700-meter- (22,000-foot-) high sacred Kailas mountain, which stands in majestic beauty apart from the Himalayan range; to all Buddhists and Hindus its peak is the center of the world, and their most devout wish is to make a pilgrimage to it. Or the honey-seekers in Kyirong: were not those honeycombs hidden in the deep gorge under an overhanging rock a miracle? Or all those animals which exist only in Tibet, and which did not become extinct because Buddhism forbids the taking of life? I am thinking of the white wild asses, the *kyangs*, which appear on the horizon like clouds and disappear again. Or the millions of migrating birds that black out the sky as they pass overhead.

Hermitages cling to sheer vertical rock faces, seemingly inaccessible, yet providing shelter and solitude for their pious visitors who, for the next three years, will not step out from the darkness of their cells which they illuminate with the light of their faith. Milarepa lived thus and wrote his magnificent mountain poems there, and they have housed numerous other saints of whom hardly any are known. There is no need to invent anything, the way those who have never experienced Tibet do. There are so many miraculous things there, things that are true, and those who seek will find them. Lhasa, though, will never be the same again; its name, "Place of the Gods," no longer applies. There is, for instance, a notice board in the center of the city depicting a horse's head: Riding Prohibited. This is a totally pointless sign nowadays because there are no horses left in the city where, once upon a time, everybody rode on horseback, where servants with their red hats, mounted like their masters, escorted the nobles, whose wives had protected their faces against the sun with a *kesang*, a little canopy. When the first Chinese arrived with their trucks the horses bolted, and that was probably when the sign was erected.

When I was living in Lhasa thirty years ago, I determined to spend the rest of my life among these peaceful and cheerful people. It was an irony of fate that just here, "on the roof of the world," it was impossible to live aloof from war and politics. Tibet had shut itself away in the belief that, so long as it existed for itself, it would also be left alone by others and would be able to live quietly and contentedly for its religion. Chinese greed for power was to devastate the country—but even though Lhasa will never rise again in the old sense, the hardworking and intelligent Tibetans are certain to polish their *norbu*, their precious stone, into a jewel again.

Norbu to me is synonymous with a country which, with all the peculiarities I have described, may yet become the greatest miracle of all—crowned by the hope that the Central Tibetans together with West and South Tibetans, but above all with the Khampas, will jointly and proudly populate their city.

6

THRONE
OF THE GODS

Amidst the many disappointments I suffered during my stay in Lhasa there was also a real ray of sunshine: Sherpa Tenzing Norgay. The first conqueror of Mount Everest accompanied the American part of our group as an additional attraction. Whenever possible we joined up, virtually clinging to one another. Tenzing, who had been to Lhasa several times since Tibet was opened up for tourism, was able to give me a lot of good advice. Although not a photographer himself, he was accurately informed on where taking pictures was permitted, where it was particularly expensive, and where it was forbidden. Tenzing today is a man famous throughout the world, and anybody at all interested in these things knows of his great achievement: the first ascent of Everest with the New Zealander Sir Edmund Hillary.

It was not always thus. When Tenzing discovered the "Valley of Flowers" with Frank Smythe in 1937 he was merely one of many porters. The same was true when, together, they made an attempt on Everest from the north, from the Tibetan side, reaching a height of 8,500 meters (28,000 feet). In this connection mention should be made of the Thirteenth Dalai Lama, who in 1910 had fled from the Chinese and gone to Darjeeling in India. Out of gratitude for the hospitality of the British administration he made what cannot have been an easy gesture, given his religious attitude: he gave the British permission to climb Everest from the north.

Tenzing was one of those Himalayan pioneers who at a very early date climbed without rope, without crampons and without oxygen. These details were never discussed in those days; that was simply how things were done then. In 1948, when he traveled to Lhasa with Professor Giuseppe Tucci, an outstanding Tibetologist, Tucci encouraged him to have another go at Everest with the British, not just as a porter but as one who would, as an equal, attempt the summit. That way he could make a name for himself. I made Tenzing's acquaintance in Lhasa then, together with Tucci, and we agreed that one day we would jointly climb Kangchenjunga.

In 1951, when I was fleeing from the Red Chinese to India via Sikkim, I asked the royal family in Gangtok, with whom I was acquainted, if they would remember Sherpa Tenzing and me if ever they gave permission for an ascent of "Kanch." The main reason why I was anxious to climb that mountain was that Peter Aufschnaiter and Paul Bauer had got close to the summit in 1929 and 1931, and the former would have wished to be one of our party. The King of Sikkim replied: "You of all people, Henrig, should understand that we do not wish anyone to go up there because, as you well know, our guardian god Kangchenjunga resides there." (The name means "the five treasures of the great snow.") Besides, the King told me, they had agreed with the Nepalese government that any such permission could only be granted in consultation between them since the summit marked the frontier between the two kingdoms. Years later I read in the paper that a British expedition had climbed "Kanch." I was deeply disappointed and inquired in Gangtok why Tenzing and I had been forgotten. The answer was that the British had promised the Nepalese to leave the summit of the mountain untouched. Of course, we would have willingly given the same undertaking. Today these problems have ceased to exist, since no one takes any account of religious or ethical values.

When I got to India after fleeing from Tibet, Tenzing—incidentally the son of a woman from Lhasa and a father from Rongbuk, at the foot of Mount Everest—had become a famous figure. With Hillary he had been the first to stand on the highest mountain in the world. Today, Everest has been climbed so often that people have stopped counting the climbers who have reached the summit. I believe, however, that it is useful to report briefly on the climbs made from the Tibetan side, from the north. Publicity was given to a "Chinese" expedition—and there is no doubt that the Chinese are firstrate mountaineers and probably even better organizers. To equip and direct such an expedition is undoubtedly an enormous feat. If, however, one looks at the names of the nine climbers who have reached the summit from Tibet, one finds that eight of them are Tibetans, even though the statistics may list them as Chinese. They include a woman, Panthog, then the best Tibetan climber. Now she has grown fat and unattractive and is married to a Chinese. Her companions on Everest were: the Tibetans Sonam Norbu, Lotse, Samdrub, Dar Puntso, Pasang, Tshering, Ngapo, and the Chinese Hou Sheng-fu. The girl Yangchenla, who looked after us at the Lhasa Guest House, had also, as a porter, reached 8,000 meters (26,000 feet) on Everest.

The history of ascents on 8,000-meter (26,250-foot) peaks in the Himalayas begins with the Frenchman Maurice Herzog. In one of the Royal Geographical Society's publications he had read Peter Aufschnaiter's account of Dhaulagiri, illustrated by my drawings. He decided to attempt the mountain, but failed and thereupon switched to nearby Annapurna, which he climbed with his expedition—the first 8,000-meter peak to be conquered in the history of mountaineering.* Later, under de Gaulle, Herzog became Minister of Sport; when, upon my return from Tibet, I gave a lecture at the Salle Pleyel in Paris, he introduced me to the audience. We have been friends ever since.

Another 8,000-meter peak is Nanga Parbat, known as "the Germans' mountain of destiny." It was first climbed by the Austrian Hermann Buhl, as a solo climb and without oxygen. Next came Cho Oyu, also climbed by an Austrian, Herbert Tichy, in what was probably the smallest and cheapest Himalayan expedition ever. It was also Tichy who, before the war, was forced to turn back with his Sherpa just short of the summit of 7,728-meter (25,355-foot) Gurla Mandhata. This mountain is still unclimbed. And it was Tichy again who circled the sacred Kailas mountain and was the first to take photographs of those pilgrims who covered the sacred path by measuring it with the length, and in some instances the width, of their bodies. This prostration, they believed, would ensure them a better reincarnation.

I should finally like to mention the lowest of the fourteen 8,000-meter peaks—Shisha Pangma, first climbed by Tibetans under Chinese leadership. Nowadays, when mountaineers like Kurt Diemberger and Reinhold Messner climb the 8,000-meter peaks as a matter of routine, all the above is ancient history.

On our escape Aufschnaiter and I were the first Europeans to cross the Chakhyungla Pass, carrying packs of 40 kilograms (88 pounds) at a temperature of minus 22°C (minus 8°F). Only when we had reached that wilderness did we dare to move in daylight, and we were rewarded by magnificent views. The deep blue of the vast Lake Pelgu lay before us, and behind it in the north the multicolored rocks of individual mountains rose above the plateau. To the south the entire plateau was framed by a brilliant chain of glaciers, and we were proud to know the names of two of the peaks—Gosainthan at 8,013

*See Maurice Herzog, *Annapurna* (Cape, 1952).

meters (26,289 feet) and, a little less high, Lapchikang. No pictures of them existed, and, like so many other Himalayan giants, both were still awaiting their conquerors. Although our hands were stiff with cold, Aufschnaiter took bearings of the principal peaks with our ancient compass and entered the figures. Maybe we would need them one day. I pulled out my sketchbook and with a few lines recorded the outlines of the mountains. We entered Shisha Pangma as Gosainthan on our maps.

In the east, too, near the Chinese-Tibetan frontier there are magnificent ice-capped mountains which are now being visited by numerous mountaineering teams, mainly American. This is the only place where the rare and delightful giant pandas are found. During my time in Lhasa I received many letters from zoo directors, asking me to send them one of those creatures. The highest offer was $50,000, but of course I never did. Not till after the war were these enchanting animals presented as "state gifts" to certain nations by the Chinese.

Sven Hedin spent many years exploring mainly the Kailas region of western Tibet, and his published accounts enjoy international fame. I have admired this legendary Swedish explorer since childhood and he has remained an example to me all my life. His is the only autograph I ever asked for; that was in Graz after a lecture by Hedin in the Stephaniensaal, when I was a young student. Subsequently, this admiration was to turn into friendship as a result of a lively correspondence between Lhasa and Stockholm. I owe it to Hedin that, during my seven years in Tibet, I wrote down and (for lack of film) sketched everything I saw and experienced. In one of his letters he had said:

Every word is of value . . . With admiration and enthusiasm I read your letter in which you describe your marvelous and fairy tale-like wanderings and adventures . . . It is quite simply fantastic that two Europeans have been living for years in that otherwise so hermetically closed capital of Tibet, that Mecca of the lamaist world, and that they have made themselves so well liked that they are actually being entrusted with confidential tasks . . . Yours is an opportunity, never before enjoyed by a European, to gain an insight into the intimate life of the Tibetans. I read your letters like novels, for they are reports from the destination of my old dreams . . .

Yours very sincerely,
Sven Hedin

This precious letter I had with me, well-packed on a horse, when I was fleeing to India. But when we had to maneuver our recalcitrant animals onto the huge wooden ferry to cross the Brahmaputra, the load containing the letters fell into the river. Although I managed to save the bundle I could not, unfortunately, unpack the letters there and then, and subsequently they proved to be washed out and almost illegible. In the summer of 1952, however, I was at least able to see the typed letters again. I had been invited to Stockholm for Sven Hedin's eighty-seventh birthday and, when I told him of my mishap, he went to the room where he kept his files, and under the letter H he produced our entire correspondence and gave me the copies. Those days with the great explorer, surrounded as he was by his brothers and sisters, all of whom lived to a similarly venerable age, are among the most beautiful and most exciting of my life. Time and again his sister Alma had to ask us to let the eighty-seven-year-old have a brief rest—we had so much to tell one another. Before my departure Hedin made me a present of all his books and signed them for me, including those famous studies and drawings of southern Tibet. On November 27, 1952, I was giving a lecture on Tibet at Feldkirch. That morning I had read in the paper that Sven Hedin had died peacefully the day before. In the evening, just before my lecture, the organizer handed me a letter whose author I instantly recognized by the writing, which sloped diagonally. It was dated November 16, and was clearly one of the last the great explorer had written.

To return to the Himalayas. Shisha Pangma, which Aufschnaiter and I had entered in our maps as Gosainthan, was climbed for the second time in 1980 by a German expedition under Manfred Abelein. He was the first European to bring back those shocking photos of the destroyed monastery town of Ganden. Since then, the Tibetans, on their own initiative and with their own means, have begun to restore Ganden, or rather to rebuild it; the Chinese, too, have made a financial contribution. Nowadays tourist buses go to Ganden to show off the restoration work.

As a token of gratitude for the hospitality shown to him, Abelein left his cross-country vehicle, a Mercedes-Puch, behind. But no sooner had the expedition left than a man slightly drunk on *chang,* Tibetan barley beer, wrecked the vehicle. It now stands, in need of extensive repair, in the shed of the Guest House. Incidentally, Abelein's porters were exclusively Tibetans selected by the Chinese. They are just as good as the Sherpas, which is not surprising since Sherpas are Tibetans too. They are really called *sharpas,* which means "the people who came from the east." About ten generations ago they migrated from Kham province via Lhasa to Nepal and became Nepalese citizens. But their religion, their appearance, their customs and traditions are purely Tibetan. Sherpa Tenzing, one of that group, now lives in Darjeeling as an Indian citizen, but he has remained a Tibetan at heart. He is a practicing Buddhist, and on one of my frequent visits to his beautiful home he told me that he— together with his whole family, three sons, one daughter and his wife Dakola—had recently been to see the Dalai Lama. Tenzing's son Tagme had been sick for a long time, and Tenzing had told the

Dalai Lama about his worries. His Holiness had replied: "My name is Tenzing, your name is Tenzing, so let us call him simply Tenzing Tagme." Since that day the boy had not been sick again.

The famous Sherpa's home is full of mementos and presents, and I invariably inspect them. On my last visit he proudly showed me a beautiful old and very rare *thangka* with a wheel of life; he had been given it in London when he was honored for his first ascent of Everest. How modest he has remained is illustrated by a small incident during our time together in Lhasa. He always produced his snuff from an old battered tin which had contained photographic film. When I asked him if he had no better snuffbox he laughed and said he had been given numerous snuffboxes as presents, made of silver, or jade, or malachite—but they were too good. This one was more practical because he need not worry if he lost it. A great mountaineer and a modest person, Tenzing, with his forty honors and civic awards, must be the most decorated man in the world.

When talking of mountaineering in the Himalayas one must not forget the foremost German climber of the prewar period—Ludwig Schmaderer. "Wiggerl," as his friends called him, together with his friend H. Paidar and the Swiss Dr. Grob, made the ascent of what is possibly the most beautiful mountain in the world, Siniolchu in Sikkim, in 1938. A year later they succeeded in making the first ascent of Tentpeak, 7,365 meters (24,165 feet) high, also in Sikkim. Then the Second World War broke out and only the Swiss was able to return to his country, while Schmaderer and Paidar joined us at our prison camp at Dehra-Dun. In view of our common interests we became friends, and I clearly remember that we decided that, as soon as the war was over, we would climb all the difficult rock faces together. Although it would have been logical, I could not consider Wiggerl as a possible partner for escape because he was linked with Paidar by their joint expeditions. When in 1944, after various unsuccessful attempts to escape, Aufschnaiter and I did not return to our camp, Wiggerl and Paidar decided to follow our example. In 1945 the two managed to get through the barbed wire; taking our route, they followed the Ganges and got to the Spiti valley, from where Aufschnaiter and I had eventually reached Tibet over two 6,000-meter (20,000-foot) passes. Wiggerl and Paidar stocked up with food for the difficult trek ahead but, resting up beyond the village, worked out that their supplies would not last. Encouraged by the effortless manner in which they had made their purchases, Wiggerl returned to the village while Paidar stayed with their kit.

This, in my opinion, was the crucial mistake made by the normally circumspect Wiggerl; clearly, he had overlooked the fact that it was strictly forbidden to travel without a permit—a practice forbidden by both the British and the Tibetan authorities. One purchase might be explained away, and the villagers could pretend not to have seen the strangers, but no such excuse would be credible on a second visit to the store. Probably both of them underrated the risk. At any rate, the sad fact is that Wiggerl was treacherously murdered—stoned to death. His corpse was left lying on the riverbed.

Wiggerl had had premonitions of his death. More than once he had said to me: "Just look at my teeth! For these gold caps I'll get myself killed one day by Himalayan bandits." All that Paidar could do after Wiggerl's death was to return to the camp. Years later, when the war was over, following his old passion, mountaineering, he was climbing the Grossglockner by way of the Pallavicini cleft when a strange thing happened. He too was hit by a stone and died.

I cannot conclude this chapter without a tribute to Peter Aufschnaiter. I made my entire escape with this agricultural engineer from Kitzbühel, a marvelous person to whom I owe a great deal. He was an exceptional character, but it was difficult to make contact with him. No friend of small talk, he was taciturn, thorough, reliable and very well-read.

When we had to leave Tibet just before the Chinese invasion,

Aufschnaiter did not return to his native Austria but instead went to Nepal, where he worked for the FAO. In order to be able to move more freely about the country, he took out Nepalese citizenship. He was to regret this step later. One day, returning to Austria on leave, he was met by the customs officials on the Brenner with the words: "We know you very well, Herr Aufschnaiter, but you are a Nepali and you need an entry visa." As a genuine Tyrolese he got furious, the more so as he regarded himself as an Austrian. After some argument, of course, he was permitted to cross the frontier. The same thing happened to him again when he was traveling from the Tyrol to Bavaria. Aufschnaiter had studied in Munich and had been Secretary of the Himalayan Foundation, and thus felt at home there too. Every three years, whenever he returned to Europe on leave, he had to go through this performance, and eventually he lost his patience. He switched back to his original nationality.

He died on October 12, 1973, while on leave in Innsbruck, and is buried in Kitzbühel in a city freeman's grave. I had visited him several times in Nepal, and last met him at a meeting of mountaineers and expedition leaders in Darjeeling. Every nation there reported on its successes in the Himalayas—only Austria remained unmentioned. At the very end I got up and humbly requested permission to say a few words on behalf of my country. I was able to report that of the fourteen 8,000-meter (26,500-foot) peaks, five had been climbed first by Austrians, while no other nation scored more than one. I thought this worth recording, just as much as the fact that, of these five 8,000-meter peaks, most had been climbed without oxygen. I concluded my report with a reference to Peter Aufschnaiter, undoubtedly one of the greatest experts on the Himalayas. Not only had he been a member of both the 1929 and 1931 Kangchenjunga expeditions, but he had an unequaled knowledge of the geography of the region. Hardly anyone spoke as many Himalayan dialects as he, or had worked there professionally for decades.

7

MILAREPA—
THE FIRST POET
OF THE MOUNTAINS

One of the most marvelous lyrical poets of the mountains lived and wrote here in the Himalayas. He is probably the most important and the best-known Tibetan saint. He lived in the eleventh and twelfth centuries in various caves between Mount Everest and Dhaulagiri, and if represented on a *thangka* or as a bronze, he is instantly recognized by his *mudra,* the position of his hands and fingers. His right hand is placed against his ear, as he listens to his own inner voice, and in his left he holds a dish of nettle salad, his only nourishment.

Milarepa's life story, which in old age he dictated to one of his disciples, is a masterpiece of Tibetan prose. It reveals more of the life, the feelings and the thoughts of the Tibetan people than anything that has ever been written about them. A song of praise to his hermitage on the slopes of the Himalayas is one of my favorite poems:

Hermitage amidst the solitude of mountains,
place where the marvelous jina *receive their* bhodi,
region where holy men are residing,

spot where now I am the only human!
Red-rocked Chonglung, eagles' nest,
clouds from the south are piling above you,
far below swift-running streams are snaking,
high in the air the vulture is circling;
every kind of forest tree whispers,
splendid trees sway like lissome dancers;
bees are humming their song Khorroro,
flowers exude the scent of Chillili;
birds are melodiously chirping Kyurruru,
up on red-rocked Chonglung
birds big and small are practicing their wing-beats,
monkeys big and small are practicing their leaps,
stags and does are practicing their running.
I, Milarepa, am practicing spiritual powers,
spiritual powers and inner holiness I practice;
with the local deity of the hermitage
I am in peaceful harmony.
Specters of evil who are assembled here
imbibe the juice of love and of mercy
and depart from hence, each to his place!

While escaping with Peter Aufschnaiter from the Indian prison camp we passed a rock monastery near the village of Kyirong Dzong. We were deeply impressed to see numerous red temples and monks' cells clinging to the rock face some 200 meters (650 feet) above the valley. We climbed the slopes, in spite of the danger of avalanches, and once again enjoyed the magnificent panorama of the Himalayas. We met a few monks and nuns, and were told by them that this was Milarepa's monastery, where the saint lived some eight hundred years ago. The monastery was called Trakar-Taso, which means "white rock of the horse's tooth." It was obvious that this magnificent setting and unique position could stimulate a receptive mind to meditation and poetry. We found it difficult to leave the place. And, having made sketches of the various monastery buildings, we determined to come back one day.

Some time ago, on a trek in the Langtrang Himalayas in northern Nepal, I met a few people from Kyirong who had lived near the monastery. They were refugees, and they told me that Milarepa's hermitages had not been destroyed. When the hordes of Red Guards came down from Dzonga-Dzong, preparing to sack the Kyirong monasteries, including the famous Samtenling, they bivouacked in the valley below the monastery, intending to start their devastation the following morning. There was a thunderstorm during the night and the plain was flooded. The river overflowed its banks, the Chinese were unable to cross the floods; Trakar-Taso was thus saved by divine intervention.

After one of my regular annual visits to the Dalai Lama at Dharamsala, he said to me as I took my leave: "Tell me, Henrig, what would give you pleasure? What wish do you have?" I replied: "No, this time you are the refugee, it's for you to make a wish." The Dalai Lama retorted: "You know quite well what I mean. Wouldn't you like a bronze or a *thangka?*" I answered: "Yes, I've been looking for a *thangka* of Milarepa. If ever you found one I should be very happy." Almost a year later, when we met again at Geneva airport on one of his visits to Europe, he came down the gangway with a roll under his arm. He said: "I've been unable to find an old *thangka* of Milarepa, so I had one painted for you . . ."

It hangs in my study to this day, and on my desk I have a valuable antique bronze of Tse-pame, the god of eternal life—another present from the Dalai Lama, which he had handed to me with the words: "Let this be your personal guardian deity."

THE DALAI LAMA IN INDIA,
THE CHINESE IN TIBET

The escape from the Chinese was accomplished in the spring
of 1959. Hundreds of journalists and thousands of believers
awaited the Dalai Lama at Tezpur (Assam province, India). I too had
gone there, representing *Life* and the *Daily Mail*. I shall never forget
the moment when the Dalai Lama suddenly spotted me among
the crowd of people and exclaimed: *"Dogpo, dogpo!"*—"Friend,
friend!"

Once in India, the Dalai Lama was interned on the instructions of
Premier Nehru, who was then still wholly on China's side. Meanwhile, life for the Tibetan people up on the roof of the world was becoming increasingly difficult. They were no longer allowed to roam
about—an unthinkable restriction for a nomadic people—and there
were no more religious holidays, which had been such an essential
part of their lives. Even the Panchen Lama, initially wooed by the
Chinese, was relieved of his office in 1964 and placed under house
arrest in Peking as a traitor. Not until June 1982 was he permitted to
see Lhasa again.

The Red Guards entered Lhasa in 1966 and perpetrated new

atrocities against the population. All animals were shot, even the birds in the air—sacrilege to Buddhists. Anything Tibetan was to be eradicated and forgotten as quickly as possible: first the language, then the fine colorful clothes, and even the fancifully plaited pigtails. Everything that had been cheerful was to be gray and depressing. The population was systematically infiltrated by Chinese, in accordance with a precise plan. In Lhasa the ratio was 120,000 Chinese to 40,000 Tibetans. Of the 3,800 monasteries and shrines only thirteen were spared, including the emblem of the city, the Potala. According to some reports, Chou En-lai prevented even worse outrages by placing regular troops on guard duty outside surviving temples: armed soldiers were regarded with respect even by the Red Guards.

Mao died in 1976 and the Chinese at last began to realize that mistakes had been made. Teng Hsiao-ping, the General Secretary of the Communist Party, made the first attempts to persuade the Dalai Lama to return to Tibet. But the Dalai Lama had learned to distrust the Chinese and demanded that a delegation of his own choosing should first visit Tibet to report their impressions to him. He sent his brother Lobsang Samten and his sister Pema Gyalpo, in separate delegations, into the occupied country. Then something happened that no one would have thought possible: the Tibetans gathered in huge numbers to convey to the sixteen emissaries of their Lama-king their tokens of love and their expressions of despair—heedless of the bewildered Chinese. Thirty years of hard and brutal Chinese oppression had failed to shake their profound faith. Secretly they produced their prayer wheels from their hiding places, brought out *khatas,* wept and touched the visitors. It was a demonstration of allegiance such as no one had dreamed of. So great was the crush that they broke down the barriers erected by the Chinese in order to be blessed by the Dalai Lama's representatives.

The Chinese were shocked when they realized that the Tibetans had remained a religion-based national unit, led by a Dalai Lama of exceptional charisma. After all, forced reeducation of other minorities, in Mongolia and Manchuria, for instance, had been reasonably successful. Now the Chinese suddenly had to admit that they had applied the wrong method to the Tibetans. True enough, they did not as a result make any concessions to them on the issue of autonomy, but they did introduce certain relaxations. In June 1980 they devised a program of reforms that was to grant the Tibetans self-determination and self-administration. They would now be able to decide for themselves what crops they wanted to grow, and they would be free to sell their harvest surpluses. They were once more allowed to cultivate their own plots of land and to keep yaks and sheep. It was promised that eighty percent of the 200,000 Chinese would leave Tibet by 1982, and those remaining were advised to learn the Tibetan language. Correspondence with the outside world was again permitted, and frontier controls were eased to allow Tibetans to visit relatives in exile.

What remained unchanged, however, was the claim that Tibetans were citizens of China. New delegations from the Dalai Lama traveled to Tibet and conducted open discussions with the Peking government; these indicated that the Dalai Lama was interested in talks about his return. Each time a new delegation came to the country, the Chinese witnessed the same demonstration of devotion and love for the Dalai Lama. The Chinese were perplexed by the Tibetans' steadfast attitude and they warned them in the (now familiar) words: "Do not forget that the Dalai Lama's emissaries are like white cranes, they come and they go. But you are like frogs in the well, and you have to remain." Considering the Tibetan people's reaction to his emissaries, it does not bear thinking about what might happen if the Dalai Lama himself were to return one day.

I have no wish to search old history books to prove exactly when Tibet was independent and when it was not. An objective answer would always be difficult, since judgment would depend on the author—on whether he was British, Indian, Tibetan or Chinese. Each one has his own version. The important question today is what it is open for Tibet and the Dalai Lama to do, and, most importantly, what concessions the Chinese are prepared to make in order to restore humane conditions. I myself am thinking of the Bhutan model. A proud and independent people, but aware of the value of India's friendship, Bhutan's representatives sit in the United Nations as an independent country but they are relieved of the worries of having to defend themselves, alone, against other powers. Another example would be Outer Mongolia, a country inhabited by a happy nomadic people, lying within the Soviet sphere of influence but with a formally independent existence as the Mongolian People's Republic and likewise with representatives in the UN.

Lobsang Samten told me on one occasion that there were approximately six million Tibetans, but about one-third of them lived outside the borders defined by the Chinese, in autonomous republics. I had myself observed that in Lhasa the Chinese army had between three and five Tibetans to every 100 Chinese, so as to ensure that the Tibetans, who do not speak Chinese, can talk to each other. To this Lobsang replied: "I am not familiar with these figures, but in all the villages there are People's Army garrisons consisting exclusively of Tibetans. They collaborate with the Chinese because the Chinese have guns." There is a strong Tibetan underground movement. In the Shugtri-Lingka park, for instance, where I used to pick wild asparagus with the Nepalese ambassador, Tibetan underground fighters wrecked the administration building where the Chinese kept their records on all Tibetans. The building was rebuilt, but the card indexes had been destroyed. Lobsang observed: "Each time something happens in town or out in the country the news spreads among Tibetans like wildfire, even without newspapers or radio." Since then the Yütok house, where I used to live, has also been burned down. It contained Chinese offices, which is why the Tibetans set fire to it.

This was the situation when I arrived back in Lhasa in the spring of 1982. Alien rule over Tibet has now gone on for three decades. A great inner disquiet and despair had swept across the Asian plateau like an elemental force, scattering Tibetan refugees to all points of the compass. Since then, as reported, conditions have somewhat improved, especially with regard to religion, but the Dalai Lama still lives in exile. The Peking government's concessions are insufficient, self-administration for Tibet is being refused, and there can be no question of independence.

In order to grant autonomy to Tibet, as provided for in the seventeen-point program of 1951, China will probably have to make further concessions. Every visitor to Tibet can see the trouble the Chinese are having with this unusual people. They have had a lot of surprises during their thirty years' occupation of Tibet, and they are ultimately affected by the age-old lure of the name of Tibet. The world public, if not its governments, will take note of the guarantees the Chinese give the Dalai Lama. There is no such thing as a bamboo curtain around Tibet; that was clear even during the cultural revolution. There have always been some leaks from Tibet to the outside world.

The high charges made by the Chinese today for visits to Tibet are likewise connected with the lure of Tibet. Tourists dreaming of Shangri-la are willing to spend a lot of money on their dream. Their disappointment is great when they discover that, apart from the Potala, the colors of the landscape and the charm of the people, nothing is left of the old enchantment. The outward destruction of a culture—destruction encountered at every step—is far worse than the abolition of the theocratic feudal system. That was something which progressive and wise Tibetans, including the Dalai Lama, had wanted to do themselves, but without the use of force.

At present negotiations are still in progress, and the Dalai Lama can afford to wait. In consequence, there is no immediate prospect of the return of the approximately 100,000 Tibetans living in exile. But do they want to return to their old homeland? The 40,000 to 50,000 Tibetans settled in southern India are said to be anxious to return, nearly all of them, even though they have put down new roots and, thanks to their adaptability and hard work, have found accommodation and own their fields. Unlike the Chinese, the Indians have long since discovered how valuable the Tibetans are to them. Schools have been built for them, and many thousands of Tibetan refugee children attend them at Indian government expense. The men are recruited into the army and, like the famous Gurkha crack units, are employed in the Himalayas and even in the disturbances in Nagaland. Time and again I have been assured by Indian friends: "The Tibetans are exceptionally hardworking and efficient people." Somehow they have all done well for themselves, and there are no poor Tibetans in India nowadays. India is thus setting a good example of how to treat minorities sensibly.

On an Indian internal flight we were looked after by a young Tibetan flight attendant in the attractive colorful costume of her homeland. She lived in Darjeeling. How much more pleasing this attire would have been also on that flight from China to Tibet, instead of those ugly plain uniforms worn by pretty young stewardesses! How pretty and natural a picture it would be if in the hotels, where members of minorities are often employed as receptionists, they were allowed to dress as they would in their native land!

Whether the Tibetans living in Switzerland, or their compatriots in Germany where they have often achieved academic positions, would be equally ready to return to their country is a difficult question. I have some doubts. But since the Tibetans in Europe are for the most part educated and intelligent people, I have been assured by the ones I have questioned that they would readily put their knowledge at the Dalai Lama's disposal and would, at least for a time, return to Tibet with him. There is no doubt that all of them would follow him if he wished them to do so.

The Tibetans who have lived in Europe for twenty-five years and have done well for themselves would certainly not find it easy to give up their affluence. Yet there is the encouraging evidence of Tibetans having time and again made themselves available whenever the Dalai Lama has needed an ambassador, and of having discharged these duties superbly. I am thinking of George Taring or of Sadutsang Rinchen, who only asked permission to follow their own interests again when they had served the Dalai Lama for a number of years. Of course, it would be easier for the older people to return to Tibet than for the youngsters who were born in Switzerland and, in some cases, hardly speak any Tibetan. But those, on the other hand, who have been shunted about for a couple of decades would be happy to return—for example, the 4,000 who fled to Bhutan and who were later refused continuing asylum unless, as the government in Thimpu demanded, they took out Bhutan nationality.

In Switzerland and in India there are a few young hotheads who have written violence on their banners. These people, too, need to be understood; certainly their wish to reconquer Tibet is not lacking in courage or in idealism. But I prefer to side with those moderate and more realistic young Tibetans who hope to regain their homeland by patience and moral claims. These young people set up the "Young Tibetans in Europe" association in the spring of 1970. It was founded in Switzerland with the object of preserving and cultivating the Tibetan cultural heritage and to keep in sight, as the principal goal, the idea of returning to a self-administered Tibet. In addition, an understanding is fostered of the culture of the host country which, after all, has become a second homeland for many of them. Whether they live in exile in India, Switzerland, America, Japan, England, Germany or Sweden, they have certainly learned that there are ideals for which it is worth working. No doubt they also realize that resignation has to be learned—it is a virtue which we in the Western world of materialism and affluence have often lost. These young Tibetans have to defend a heritage that is spiritually superior to ours; they must protect and safeguard it. They are the ones with the opportunity to make comparisons, to realize that material values alone are meaningless and that, on the other hand, one can no longer live only for the sake of religion and outdated forms of government. That is precisely why these people, the youngsters in exile, are predestined to follow the Dalai Lama if his hoped-for return to Tibet comes to pass. After all, our European youngsters are likewise desperately searching for models and for a meaning to life. They travel to Dharamsala and seek the solution to their problems in the Dalai Lama's vicinity. It is precisely the Tibetan form of Buddhism, magnanimous and open-minded as it is, that might bring succor to the pessimism of the West.

Meanwhile, the number of artisan centers where Tibetan exiles are working has risen to twelve. Production of bronzes by ancient methods, painting of *thangkas* and carpetmaking—all these may help to preserve and propagate thousand-year-old cultural traditions. These centers dispatch their products to every corner of the earth, and many European shops carry Tibetan manufactures as a matter of course.

9

THE CHILDHOOD OF
A THIRTEEN-YEAR-OLD

Lobsang Tempa is thirteen and lives in the Tibetan Institute in Rikon in Switzerland. He is a healthy and contented young Tibetan refugee, but I felt some reservations about questioning him on events which might sadden him. Cautiously I approached him about his past, and I was surprised at the clarity of his recollections and the matter-of-fact manner of his account.

The Chinese, Lobsang Tempa told me, had divided the population into three main categories. The first of these were the Tibetans wooed by the Chinese, the "two-headed ones," as the people called them, the collaborators. They and their families enjoyed numerous privileges: they could go to school and to university, they were allowed to improve their qualifications by studying in Peking, and of course they got the best jobs in the administration. Their salary was in the region of 80 to 100 *yüan*, approximately $45 to $50 per month.

The large number of Tibetans in the second category, those who—like Lobsang Tempa's parents—did not wish to commit themselves publicly to either side, who were neither pro-Chinese nor nationalistically Tibetan, had a pay of about 40 *yüan* ($23). Lobsang Tempa had been allowed to attend school; his textbooks had been Tibetan books in printed characters and he had written not with traditional bamboo sticks but with steel nibs in cursive script. Lessons had been from Monday to Friday. On Saturday, in the afternoons, the pupils had to clean the school. As for their clothes, the boy of thirteen had this to say: "One got praise from the Chinese if one dressed shabbily, with a lot of patched-up scraps of cloth, and as drably as possible, in gray or blue. That way one was considered thrifty and one was popular with one's teachers." In consequence the classes looked "uniform," and nobody dared to wear the pretty and colorful materials or aprons of Tibetan national dress. Lobsang Tempa was a pupil of what was called the "First Chinese School," attended by 1,300 children, with Tibetans and Chinese having separate instruction. During the physical training period, however, they played football against each other. But the most important feature was the joint military gymnastics in the early morning.

Lobsang Tempa left Lhasa in December 1979, together with his parents, on a pilgrimage to India. He was therefore still in India at the time of the visiting delegation under Lobsang Samten, the Dalai Lama's brother, but no longer when Pema Gyalpo, the Dalai Lama's sister, arrived. Before the first visit the children had been strictly forbidden at school to stare at the delegates, let alone to accept presents from them. I have already described what in fact did happen. (The Chinese, incidentally, similarly prepare the population for tourist visits.)

The third category consists of those Tibetans who gallantly defended their independence. These were predominantly nobles, seminobles and lamas; they were punished by being made to perform the lowliest tasks, such as laboring on roads and bridges. They were further humiliated by being made to clean up the city before the tourists arrived; they were subsequently packed into trucks and kept out of sight while the first tourists and, more important, the Dalai Lama's delegation arrived. There was a camp for these outcasts a short distance east of Lhasa—Tsal Gungthang—originally for beggars and vagrants. It was set up before the arrival of the Dalai Lama's first delegation, as part of the deception practiced on them and on the tourists.

I should like to observe here that there were at least 2,000 beggars in Lhasa in my day, but they never suffered hunger because they were real "professionals" at their job. No Tibetan would ever have refused them alms, even if only a spoonful of flour. The Chinese were anxious to prove that there were no longer any poor people or beggars in the streets.

Members of the third category of Tibetans received only something like 35 *yüan* ($20) per month. A new word emerged in Tibetan: *Thabzing*—a synonym for mental cruelty and destruction of all human dignity. Whenever Tibetans in that group returned home in the evening, *Thabzing* began—we would call it brainwashing. At 7 P.M., Lobsang Tempa continued, they were all called together for a session of indoctrination. One of them had to stand in front of the others, and they had to accuse him, spread slanders about him, and in the end he was compelled to accuse himself. The delinquents were reviled, kicked and beaten. Each person had his turn in this ghastly performance. Some families preferred suicide rather than undergo that kind of treatment. Parents were forced to watch the execution of their older children, sentenced to death for working in the resistance, and to applaud. Children were forced to cheer.

After these *Thabzing* atrocities one begins to understand those Tibetans who denied their families and even their faith, and who often acted even worse than the Chinese. The Hamburg psychiatrist Professor Bürger-Prinz had said of brainwashing that every person has a point beyond which he cannot be stressed.

Calmly and without dramatizing the boy told me about life in Lhasa. He seemed almost embarrassed to find me listening so seriously to his account and accepting his impressions and conclusions as my own.

Not all Tibetans are able to forget the atrocities of the revolution: hence their understandable mistrust of a reported "thaw." They also view with a mixture of mistrust and hope the repeated Chinese assurances that the Dalai Lama will return by the end of the year. This is indispensable Chinese propaganda, since they know full well that they cannot control the Tibetans without the Dalai Lama.

On the flight from Lhasa to Peking I read an interview in a Chinese paper, given by Hu Yao-pang, the Chairman of the Communist Party, to an American professor of Columbia University. Among other things he confessed that the Chinese had been taught a thorough lesson in Tibet and had drawn their conclusions from it. No one attempting to break the will of a people could ever succeed. Over the ten years from 1966 to 1977 the Chinese themselves in their homeland had been greatly impoverished, and never again would they act so stupidly. In the words of Hu Yao-pang: "I have once knocked my nose against the wall, but it will not happen a second time."

What do the Tibetans think of this? The Chinese have lost too much credibility over the years. This was also confirmed to me every day in Lhasa by their "Potemkin villages"—the pretense sustained, for example, by butter and meat being available only in Lhasa, while outside the city people were going hungry, or by the sham repairs to monasteries performed solely for the benefit of tourists' cameras.

10

REFLECTIONS
ON TIBET'S FUTURE

Are these amiable people then doomed to drift along like sheep without a shepherd? In all my conversations, I observed that even some responsible Chinese believed that their atrocities and devastations represented no more than a senseless explosion which had blown up cultural treasures, driven the gifted Lama-king out of the country, and replaced him, amidst the ruins, the debris and the dust, with a multiplicity of incompetent "disguised" rulers. Certainly, avarice, corruption and incompetence had existed also among Tibetan regents. But they had been sentenced or deposed, for there had been an orderly system, there had been good ministers, scholars and cultured monks, not strangers governing by virtue of superior strength and brute force. The Tibetans I talked to were all convinced that they could once more govern themselves, that they could manage on their own. What they sought was justice; that was what Tibet needed. All of them, both in Lhasa and in exile, were hoping that the day was not too far off—even though it still needed a change of attitudes—when order would return to Tibet. One can hardly ask these people to be patient; they have been almost too patient. But I believe they must not lose hope, for hope is life.

The Chinese should not make things too easy for themselves, either vis-à-vis the Tibetans or vis-à-vis the outside world, by always blaming everything on the Gang of Four. These politicians had indeed been the rulers of Tibet, but all the damage they had done had been in the name of the Chinese people. Are the Tibetans expected suddenly to reverse their way of thinking and to believe that the Chinese wish to show tolerance to the refugees whom, until not so long ago, they treated as traitors and criminals? Evidently they are not quite sure themselves how this is to be done. For the present they still differentiate between Tibetans who fled the country in 1959 and those who stayed behind. Those who collaborated with the Chinese are given preferential treatment and privileges. If the exiles were to return from India, Switzerland and elsewhere, they would probably be treated as second-class citizens. But these are the very people who could be of great value to Tibet with all the information and new knowledge they have acquired during their stay abroad.

I had an opportunity to discuss this subject with a senior Chinese official in Lhasa; he saw my point, agreed with me, and promised to report to Peking accordingly. I have also had a conversation with the Chinese ambassador in Vienna, who declared to me positively that there would be no discrimination in the future, and that the Dalai Lama was welcome. However, a little time must be allowed to elapse, which is exactly what the Tibetans also want. The Chinese must realize that the Tibetans abroad fled from the very situation that they, the Chinese, now claim to be condemning themselves— the cultural revolution under the evil Gang of Four.

My old friend Wangdü, whose fate I shall report on in a later chapter, told me that a Refugee Restitution Office was already in existence and that anybody could go there for advice. He also told me that some ancient noble families who had stayed behind in Tibet were once among the richest people in the country; although the Chinese were not returning any lands to them, they were paying them restitution in money. Naturally, to be rich in a communist country does not mean quite the same as it does to us in the West. The expropriated estates are now communes, where Tibetans work under Chinese supervision. There are a few machines, also an occasional motor vehicle, but wherever I look the Tibetans work with their hands. I observe hardly any difference from the old days, except that a small donkey cart is jogging along the track on rubber tires—a novelty such as the wheel was not common in everyday life in Tibet. It had in fact been forbidden for daily use; this was on religious grounds. An ancient Tibetan prophecy states: "With the wheel comes the end." The Thirteenth Dalai Lama had in fact tried to utilize the wheel, but each time he had come up against the power of the monks. Today the wheel has lost much of its significance as a sacred religious symbol.

Much is as it was before; some things are worse, a few things are better. The yak is still the most useful animal in agriculture. In the communes, triangular red pennants adorn the animals' foreheads, whereas Tibetans used to decorate their yaks with red-stained yaks' tails. On a few occasions I saw cowrie shells decorating the animals' foreheads. Progress will be slow and laborious, there can be no doubt about that, and for a while there will still be poverty and hardship—but then tranquillity and faith, Tibet's true characteristics, will return. That is my hope and belief.

It is obvious to anyone who knows Tibet that the most pressing need of that vast country is communications. Without roads there can be no modern administration in such a large territory. This is realized by Tibetans, and even during my time there the issue was discussed in the Kashag, the Council of Ministers. Ideas and projects existed even then, but unfortunately they were never realized, possibly because there was no agreement on whether public benefit came before private profit. Today, the Chinese claim to be the originators of all reforms, whether in medicine, education or land allocation. Now that these are being introduced from outside, they encounter some resistance on the part of the Tibetans, who do not take advice kindly at the best of times.

An educated Tibetan once told me that his people would have to recover their balance first, since no nation on earth had been treated worse than they had. They had been caught up in a vortex of events they did not understand, and yet they had persevered with unflinching application, faith and patience, and surely this attitude would triumph in the end. But not the way the Chinese have gone about it—by introducing harvesting machinery so that more wheat can be grown, which has then been transported to China to feed the Chinese. Much the same is true of the railway which, like the bridges and roads, serves the military purposes of the invaders rather than the interests of the Tibetans.

Yak-hide boats, which had been the means of river travel, have become quite rare now. On the Brahmaputra I spotted one such boat, engaged in fishing, and I questioned its occupants about their work. In the days of the Dalai Lama, fishing had been forbidden. Now there are professional fishermen, whose catches supplement the Tibetans' food supplies.

Aufschnaiter and I had occasionally broken the fishing ban and collected some tasty fish from the Nepalese ambassador's Gurkha bodyguard, who often fished in secret. Gurkha soldiers then enjoyed a certain notoriety in Lhasa for their brazen disregard of the ban on fishing. Whenever news reached the government, a protest was lodged with the Nepalese embassy and this marked the beginning of a pleasant game. The Nepalese representatives attached great importance to good relations with the Lhasa government, so the malefactors had to be punished. Of course, this was just a formality and the government was satisfied. No one apart from the Gurkhas, however, would have dared to go fishing in those days. In the whole of Tibet there was just one locality which enjoyed fishing rights. This was on the Tsangpo, in a sandy desert unsuitable for arable or livestock farming. There was no grazing whatever, and fish were therefore the only source of food, which explained the exception. Admittedly, as a result, the population of the village was regarded as inferior, as indeed were the guilds of butchers and blacksmiths.

I can only repeat that it was generally agreed, in the old days in Lhasa, that there would have to be many changes in the country, where the government was a blend of feudalism and ecclesiastical politics, rather like Europe in the Middle Ages.

When I was writing my book *Seven Years in Tibet,* I was particularly concerned to make my account so accurate and truthful that neither Peter Aufschnaiter nor Hugh Richardson, both of whom had witnessed it all, could accuse me of errors or exaggeration. But it never occurred to me that my portrayal of the Tibetan people would one day be open to verification all over the world. Goethe says in *Maximen und Reflektionen:* "Before the great merits of others there is no salvation but love . . ."—and it was certainly love that made me portray the Dalai Lama and his people the way I did. Thus it was a wonderful experience to find that, when hundreds of thousands of Tibetans had fled to foreign lands, they were praised everywhere for their diligence and their adaptability.

Efforts are under way on all sides to find a solution. Even the Chinese seem to be seeking a way out, though it has taken them a long time to understand that the Tibetans' reaction is totally different from the one they had expected. First of all, the Chinese had to get over their shock at the incidents associated with the visit of the Dalai Lama's delegation and with the return of the Panchen Lama. That took them the best part of two years. They tried to play it down by explaining—as, incidentally, Wangdü did—that the overwhelming reception had been due solely to religious and certainly not to political motives. A period of quiescence ensued, and no invitation was made to the Dalai Lama to return to Tibet. Not until April 6, 1982, when I was in Lhasa, did the important *China Daily* carry the following report on its front page under the headline "Dalai Lama Invited to Return Home for Good?" I am quoting it in an abridged form:

> "The Dalai Lama and his followers, who are at present living abroad, are free to visit relatives and settle in China at any time. We promise that they are also free to leave again." This statement was made by the First Secretary of the Communist Party of the Autonomous Republic of Tibet, Yin Fatang, at a meeting of the local workers' party. He said: "It is the policy of our party not to rake up the past, not to stir up what has happened, but to look to the future." He added that the Dalai Lama and his followers should have trust in China's policy, and he expressed the hope that they would make their contribution to their mother country's amalgamation into a family of all nationalities and to its modernization. If they harbored any doubts, they could wait and watch developments from outside for a few more years. He concluded: "The families in Tibet of our comrades at present abroad are certainly enjoying the same treatment as the rest of the Tibetan people."

Although, in his modest way, the Dalai Lama keeps emphasizing that his person is unimportant, I am bound to say that this is not the case. Indeed, I believe it to be of decisive importance. The Chinese experiment in bringing the Panchen Lama to Lhasa revealed the reaction of the Tibetan people. Although the Panchen Lama has nothing like the charisma of the Dalai Lama, he nevertheless triggered off powerful emotions. The aura of the Dalai Lama and the deep-rooted veneration of his people give rise to an almost universal hope that he will soon resume the secular and spiritual leadership of Tibet. This was acknowledged also by the Panchen Lama when he emphatically declared that he would exercise his office only under the superior authority of the Dalai Lama, whose wisdom and ascetic life plainly predestined him for that high function. His and his people's strength, moreover, should stem not from indulging in self-accusations but from acknowledging the mistakes of the past and not committing them again. The Dalai Lama does not, according to his own statements, regard himself as a living god—this is a description used only in the West. He can be flexible and practices tolerance, the great virtue of Buddhism.

I have frequently asked myself what Tibet needs most. What would the Tibetans need to do if they were left to their own devices? Obviously, they would have to set up a transport network, without which no proper administration can function, as well as a comprehensive telephone and telegraph system, hydroelectric power stations and cement works, as originally planned by Tsarong. Mining of as yet untapped mineral resources and intensification of agricultural methods would be indispensable; these could be made possible by the construction of a power station of enormous dimensions in the Brahmaputra gorge, just where the river bursts through from the Himalayas into India. Just as important would be reforestation, neglected for centuries. All this the Chinese have promised, but it would be a vast program and so far, in spite of all the talk of reforms, it is still only on paper. As yet the Tibetans themselves are divided— the collaborators at home, the Dalai Lama's loyal followers, and the Tibetans in exile. Whenever I talked to pro-Chinese Tibetans in Lhasa I asked them: "What has really changed, what has really improved? Have not thirty years been pointlessly wasted, years that might have served reforms?"

I have mentioned Yin Fatang, the Chinese party boss in Lhasa, and his statement in the *China Daily*. This man heads a cabinet, similar to the former Kashag; where once a lama used to preside, a Chinese political functionary is now installed. Below him are three Tibetans, but they do not have much say—again very much like the Kashag, where a lama presided over three Sawangchenpos, secular ministers who ranked equal with him. A number of departments under the present-day cabinet are concerned with education, the economy, industrialization, transport and religion. There are thirteen ministries altogether. The Cultural Department is headed by my old friend Wangdü, nowadays better known by his name of Thubten Nyima. His head is full of good ideas, but they have to be approved by the Chinese first.

The Tibetans' great opportunity lies in the fact that the Han, as the Chinese are called, do not like working in Tibet at all and that, in consequence, administrative posts are gradually passing into Tibetan hands. But there is still the Chairman of the "Chinese Communist Party of the Autonomous Republic of Tibet." Not a lot, therefore, has changed. The only difference is that the cabinet now sit at a table, on chairs, and no longer on cushions of differing heights according to rank. The parallel goes even further: once more, as in the old days, there is one man at the very top, exercising power, and he and his collaborating Tibetan colleagues are again divided on whether to serve the common weal or their personal interests.

The Chinese have alleged that, under the feudal system in the Dalai Lama's day, the Tibetans worked as slaves. During my many years in Lhasa I frequently observed that whenever a servant was summoned to a household in Lhasa, this tended to raise rather than lower his status. In addition to his service he was able to engage in trade and thereby improve his standard of living. One might well ask who enjoyed greater freedom: the man working as a "slave" for a wage in the household or in the fields of his aristocratic lord, or the man eking out an existence in a Chinese labor camp.

The Chinese have denounced the high dues which the people of the Dalai Lama's feudal state had to pay. What they overlook is the fact that this was a different form of taxation, with every subject delivering a tolerable portion of what he produced or possessed—such as butter in the mountain pasture areas of the Himalayas, grain in the fertile valleys and wool from the nomads of the Changthang. If a family lived in an area where willows were plentiful they would make brooms and deliver those as their dues. A peasant whose small farmstead was surrounded by juniper bushes or azaleas would deliver several bundles of these for incense burning in the monasteries. Wealthy nobles and big landowners would pay their dues by performing services to the state: they raised troops among their subjects and discharged official duties without pay. A sensible and equitable arrangement, I would have thought, which by no means turned a servant into a "slave," as asserted by the Chinese. A Tibetan cutting willows and weaving baskets was certainly more free than one under the constraints of a commune.

There are other good reasons which might induce the Chinese to withdraw slowly and give the Tibetans more and more freedom. The gigantic cost of the occupation must play an important part: transport of foodstuffs, pay for the troops stationed in Tibet—a lot could be saved if Tibetans were trained for the jobs. The troops, of course, will remain—one should have no illusions on that score. But one day they will give up as hopeless the indoctrination of the Tibetans. Even now as a tourist I noticed that we were no longer made to leave the bus every few minutes—as earlier travelers had to—in order to inspect nurseries, schools or communes specially created for propaganda, and listen to the Chinese guide's commentary on the blessings of communism.

The so-called "Chamber of Horrors" at the foot of the Potala is also no longer shown. I believe that the Chinese were perfectly well aware that they were conning the tourists with displays of desiccated human arms, flutes made from femurs, and silver-mounted skulls; these objects, they used to maintain, testified to torture, flogging and other atrocities. Even Wangdü was so much under Chinese influence that he confirmed the atrocity stories spread by the Chinese about the Tibetans. He reminded me that in the days of the Fifth Dalai Lama (in the eighteenth century), and even under the Thirteenth (1900–33), Tibetans still had their hands and feet chopped off. In reply to my direct question he had to admit that this had ceased to happen during my time in Tibet.

Throughout my seven years in Tibet I witnessed only two floggings—little comparison with the cruelty that occurs in the whole world in a single day. That time, in Kyirong, it involved a nun of the reformed Buddhist church which prescribes strict celibacy. The nun had had a child by a monk of the same church, and had killed it immediately after birth. The two were reported, put in the pillory, and sentenced to 100 lashes. While this was still going on, the public, with the customary presents of money and with *khatas*, pleaded with the executing official for mercy. As a result the punishment was reduced, and a sigh of relief ran through the tightly packed crowd, many of whom were weeping. The public's compassion was amazing. Gifts of money and food were sent to both parties in great quantity, and the two left Kyirong with well-lined pockets to go on a pilgrimage.

In the second instance of flogging the circumstances had been especially tragic. When the Red Chinese occupied Turkestan, the American consul there, Mackiernan, together with a fellow countryman, a student named Bessac, and three White Russians, prepared to escape to Tibet. Via India he applied to the Tibetan government for a transit permit, and Lhasa immediately dispatched mounted messengers to the north to make sure the reinforced frontier patrols would not put obstacles in the way of the refugees. The route of their small caravan lay across the Kuen Lun and the Changthang. As ill luck would have it, the government messenger was too late reaching the spot where the American and his companions intended to cross the frontier. Before a challenge or negotiations were possible, the frontier post had opened fire. The American consul and two Russians were killed instantly. The third Russian was wounded and only Bessac escaped unhurt. He was taken prisoner and an escort set off with him and the wounded man to the nearest governor. The treatment they received was rather rough and Bessac was reviled and threatened as an invader. But before the transport with the two prisoners reached the nearest official, the messenger arrived with orders that the two Americans and their companions were to be received as guests of the government. The Tibetan soldiers became very subdued and outdid one another in courtesies. But what had been done could not be undone; three men had lost their lives.

The governor made a report to Lhasa. There was great dismay at what had happened and every possible effort was made to convey the government's regrets. An Indian-trained medical orderly was sent out with gifts for Bessac and the wounded Russian. The two were asked to come to Lhasa and appear as witnesses against the soldiers, who had already been taken into custody. In Lhasa a garden house with servants was prepared to receive the visitors. Fortunately, the injuries of the Russian Vasilev proved not to be dangerous and he soon recovered. The two stayed in Lhasa for a month, and I made friends with Bessac during that time. He harbored no ill feelings against the country which had given him such a poor welcome; the only satisfaction he demanded was that the soldiers who had treated him so badly on the journey to the governor should be punished. He was requested to attend the administration of the punishment to rule out any suspicion of deception, but when he saw the severity of the flogging he himself pleaded for mitigation. He took pictures of the scene, which were subsequently published in *Life,* so that the Tibetan government was vindicated in the eyes of the world. Bessac then moved on to the frontier with Sikkim, where representatives of his country were awaiting him.

However, what the Chinese had been displaying in the museum at the foot of the Potala were in fact relics of great artists, whose creative hands had been preserved in a spirit of veneration. This is no different from Catholic churches who also keep the skulls, bones and bodies of dead saints, embalmed and still venerated. Aprons and flutes made from bones, and silver-mounted skulls, are religious objects derived from persons who died a natural death, objects reverently used as musical instruments and cultic items during religious ceremonies. They had nothing to do with atrocities but were part of the rites of a different religion which should be approached with tolerance.

Regrettably the first few reporters who were permitted to travel in Tibet fell for these lies about Tibetan child killers and accepted everything they saw as true. The most prominent accounts were those of Han Suyin, who, without bothering to study the culture of the Tibetans, published a widely read book about their "atrocities."

Today, even the theater has ceased to present those "cruel nobles who exploited and ground the faces of the people and fettered them with heavy iron chains." The Chinese have since realized that such propaganda damaged them more than it did the Tibetans. At the same time, what is nowadays offered to tourists in Lhasa as Tibetan culture is a compound of Chinese folklore, with a slight American touch. When I criticized the hideously made-up dancers, quite unlike the old Tibetan simplicity, and asked why there was no Tibetan instrument to be found in the orchestra, I was informed: "Ah, we are progressive now." I discussed these things with Wangdü, but he did not share my dislike. He called it "national minorities music" or "national minorities instrumental music." It was new, and adapted to the tastes of the Chinese and the wider world.

I remember talking in Switzerland to a Tibetan theatrical ensemble from Dharamsala, who were trying to earn money in the West. I said to them: "Don't please imitate the Chinese in everything by portraying the terrible things they have done. Set a good example, for your religion teaches forgiveness and tolerance." Fortunately both sides have stopped these frightful theatrical performances. However, the theater in Tibet has not got any better: since Americans make up the bulk of the tourists, performances are concluded by the singing of "Jingle bells, jingle bells . . ." No turning to the gods anymore, no continuation of the great Tibetan tradition. It would be good to see a return to the religious mystery play and to sacred dances, by way of a moral guide and antidote to the utilitarian beliefs of our age—for to the Tibetans their faith and their culture represent a unity.

I shall refrain from giving the Tibetans advice. I can only see things through my subjective eyes, and besides, I know only too well that no one can give advice to Tibetans. They invariably listen with interest, but they always hold to their own views and stand by them. While I was living in Tibet, European newspapers were fond of reporting that I was their adviser or even their general. Such reports could have sprung only from total ignorance of the Tibetan character. I am not alone in experiencing how difficult it is to give them advice—the Chinese have discovered it too, and so have the British and the Indians. I cannot and I do not wish to give advice. All I can do— as in my first book, *Seven Years in Tibet*—is draw attention, time and again, to that small, gallant, lovable people, so that the world, and more especially the Chinese, recognize them, give them their freedom, and allow them their profound faith under their Dalai Lama. My wish is for a country with, once again, the lure which Tibet has always exercised and to which, of course, I too have succumbed.

When Peter Aufschnaiter and I arrived in Lhasa as poor exhausted fugitives, we were accepted without reservation by the Tibetans. We were housed, and I was nursed by them when I was seriously ill. They showed us compassion, which I can repay only by continuing to arouse sympathy for them, in the hope of showing that a nation that is so different from the Chinese and that possesses so many characteristics of its own, deserves its autonomy. Above all, I believe that it is their religion that deserves sustaining, as it is a source of inexhaustible support to them. Undoubtedly the institution of the lamaist church has committed errors, which even the Dalai Lama acknowledges. Peter Aufschnaiter was never able to conceal his dislike of the intrigues and the scheming of the ecclesiastical dignitaries: we often suffered from them while working for the government. Much needed changing in this sphere—and intelligent Tibetans realized this—but the changes needed to come from within, organically and step by step. Unassailable above everything is the person of the Dalai Lama. Numerous Tibetans I talked to assured me that for them the Dalai Lama was the only one who commanded veneration. Tenzing Norgay, the famous Sherpa, told me quite recently that he was not interested in the Panchen Lama or in any other incarnation—it was only the Dalai Lama whom he truly revered and before whom he prostrated himself.

I Am Recognized

It was the spring of 1982. Thirty years later. I was back in Lhasa, and alone at last. I had risen early and could go wherever I wished. Without a chaperon—what bliss! My time was precious and I wanted to miss as little as possible. First I strolled to Lingkhor, an eight-kilometer (five-mile) pilgrimage road around Lhasa; today it survives in sections only. I recalled our arrival in Lhasa over thirty years ago, when we were paying our courtesy calls. That time we had also gone to see the monk-minister on Lingkhor, and I now remembered his words: "In our ancient writings there is a prophecy that a great power from the north will make war on Tibet, destroy religion, and make itself master of the whole world . . ."

Lingkhor no longer exists in its old form—running through gardens full of flowers and past picturesque corners. I was surprised to see that on an asphalted road, with buses and trucks circulating, pilgrims were prostrating themselves—until I realized that I was on Lingkhor already. I saw a few stonemasons chiseling figures of deities, and some incense burners were alight in the road around a place of offerings canopied by prayer flags and guarded by an old monk. I strolled on along the transformed Lingkhor and discovered a still-delightful spot by a tributary of the Kyichu. I knew the spot well from the past, and I knew that the "Blue Buddha" was here reflected in the water's surface. Several times on this trip I asked myself if I was really in the country which for seven years had been my home—but at this spot, for the first time, I felt that, outwardly at least, nothing had changed. The faithful, passing this freshly repainted rock relief, touch the sacred rock with their foreheads, their backs and their hands—just as they had done in the past.

I stopped for a long time, until scarcely anyone was in sight. Lhasa was far away, long and weary shadows were already slipping down the rocks, and the little stream was rushing along melodiously. I discovered some leftovers of the New Year—old tins with the green sprouts of barley. I gazed up at the Blue Buddha, his left hand gripping a thunderbolt, a symbol of immutability and indestructibility. Numerous other incarnations from the lamaist pantheon surround the central divine figure, among them, enthroned, the eleven-headed Chenrezi, the "god of mercy," whose incarnation is the Dalai Lama. In the dusk the many prayer flags were weaving among the trees, and I did not find it difficult to believe that the spot was still inhabited by the spirits which guard the religion and the gods. Unlike the old days, there were hardly any beggars; only ducks beating their wings, as they had always done, whenever one of the few pilgrims fed them at this last romantic spot in Lhasa.

As I returned to that city, an almost spectral silence hung over houses and streets. A few nomads were approaching; they asked me for a picture of the Dalai Lama and told me they had been on the move for five months; they would stay a week in Lhasa. I went on until I came to Barkhor, the inner ring-road enclosing the Tsuglagkhang, the most sacred of Tibetan temples. In the old days the city's entire life was concentrated on Barkhor, where most of the shops were. I had then written in my diary:

> Barkhor has its heyday at the New Year. Here all religious cere-
> monies and processions begin and end. In the evenings, espe-
> cially on holy days, the faithful move along Barkhor in huge
> numbers; they mumble their prayers, and many of them mea-
> sure out the distance by flinging their bodies to the ground.
> Yet this inner ring-road also has a less pious aspect: pretty
> young women there display their colorful costumes, their tur-
> quoise and coral jewelry, they flirt with the nobles, and the local
> beauties of easier virtue also find there what they are after. The
> center of commerce, of social life and of gossip—that is
> Barkhor.

The Mani and lama singers no longer exist. They used to sit on the ground in the old days, a *thangka* would hang on the wall, illustrating the life of some saint, and in a singsong voice they would relate to their listeners the most wondrous tales, all the while turning their prayer wheels.

This time, too, Barkhor was swarming with people whose features radiated contentment. Many of the older women recognized me, started to cry, and asked if I could tell them anything about the Dalai Lama, or if I had a picture of him for them. I asked them how many Tibetans were still *nangpa* after thirty years of communism. *Nangpa* means "within" and it denotes people within the Buddhist faith. "About 100 percent" was their brief answer. "What's become of Po-la, the one with the beard, surely there were two of you?" They meant Peter Aufschnaiter. They offered me pots and ritual vessels of copper, brass and bronze, old and beautiful ones, which they wanted to sell for very little money, for 50 to 100 *yüan*, about the same number of Swiss francs. Dozens of young Tibetans, who could not have known me from the past, soon crowded around us. They were astonished and amused to find a stranger speaking their Lhasa dialect.

In reply to a question from me our Chinese guide had told me: "Of course you can buy those things." But everyone knew that it was forbidden, and I felt fairly sure the pots would be taken away from us before our departure. A pity, since both sides would have benefited from the transaction. And the example of other countries has shown what a blessing it was that Europeans purchased or carried off artistic treasures which would otherwise have been destroyed. Thus a few museums at least can testify today to the culture of the Tibetan people.

Here on Barkhor, at the foot of the Potala, one could just about visualize how enchanting this city was in the past. The Tibetans invariably used only stone and timber to erect their beautiful buildings. Just imagine: those blocks of granite were joined together without any cement, only with clay, and the gigantic Potala, constructed in this manner, has withstood all earthquakes.

But now the "modern age" has arrived. Following the Chinese invasion, everything was transformed except the small inner kernel of the city. All around, as far as the eye can roam, there is now a sea of hideous tin roofs. I stood on the roof of the Potala and was blinded by the ugly tin; I had to shut my eyes. The whole atmosphere of the city was gone. I talked about it to Wangdü, who is presently responsible for the maintenance of the Potala. I reminded him of the many times we had talked about building a new Lhasa with a great canal, with fresh water between Norbulingka and the Tölung valley. Aufschnaiter and I had already drawn up plans and made drawings. All the banks were to be covered with flowers, like the Hanging Gardens of Babylon, and trees were to be planted in front of the palace.

Instead, there is now this sad wasteland of tin roofs. Wangdü remembered our plans perfectly well; he assured me he would use his influence to have all the hideousness removed and instead have traditional timber-and-stone houses erected at the foot of the Potala.

The vast park of Shugtri-Lingka is also irretrievably lost. It started at the dense cluster of houses in the little village of Shö, below the Potala, where the Dalai Lama's state printing press and stabling were located, as well as the prison, and extended all the way to the Kyichu. At the center of the park stood a stone throne, Shugtri, which for certain rare ceremonies served the Dalai Lama as a seat. Here I used to walk with the Nepalese ambassador, twice a year, in order—as mentioned before—to pick asparagus. Now this too is a sea of cheap hutments and tin-roofed houses.

The Potala, the emblem of Lhasa, has survived everything—the centuries, several earthquakes and, worst of all, the destructive fury of the Red Guards. Maybe its spacious internal courtyard, where the fantastic black-hatted dancers used to perform, will again be the scene of similar events for the benefit of tourists. But never again will spectators sit at different levels of the palace, robed in precious brocade and brilliant shimmering silk: on the top floor the Dalai Lama with his three attendants; on the floor below him the solemn figure of the Regent; next the ministers, the parents of the Lama-king and the rest of his relations; finally among them, in those days, myself—staring respectfully at Tibet's high dignitaries.

Instead of brocade and silk, future spectators will wear blue-and-green uniforms, and identical caps on their heads. My unforgettable impressions of the various colorful hats, the splendid variety of garments and furs now belong to the past—only in museums will people be able to admire that pomp. There is no doubt that intelligent tourists can do something to preserve these ancient cultural values. One would need to support the Tibetans tactfully and sensitively, assuring them that it is of the utmost importance that ancient customs and rites are preserved before—as might so easily happen—it is too late. We in the West have also frequently been late—sometimes, unfortunately, too late—in realizing the importance of cultivating and safeguarding our cultural heritage.

My Old Friend
Wangdü

I shall never forget one of my first encounters with Wangdü, the senior monk-official. We were going to dine at the only Chinese restaurant in Lhasa and there, running about in the yard, saw a goose, clearly intended for the pot. Wangdü impulsively fished out a big banknote, bought the goose off the Chinese and had his servant carry it home. He had done that to save a life. For many years afterward I saw that goose waddling about, evidently enjoying a peaceful old age. Some thirty years had passed since that little episode, and all the things I have attempted to describe in the preceding chapters had happened in the meantime. Two young and carefree lads had turned into middle-aged men; both of them had tried, by very different roads and each in his own way, to give some meaning to their lives through patience and optimism. Thus, on March 5, 1982, at Lhasa airport, it was with a good deal of trepidation that I faced Drölma, Wangdü's wife, as I posed the question I had formulated so often over the previous weeks: "Is Wangdü in Lhasa and have I any hope of seeing him?" Drölma had hesitated in her reply, and in those very first minutes on Tibetan soil I realized how great was still the fear of the powerful conqueror. I had not pressed her any further but had inquired instead from our Chinese guides whether I might meet an old friend.

The reunion necessitated a laborious amount of bureaucracy. I had to apply in writing to the Lhasa branch office of Lüxingshe, the Chinese Tourist Authority, giving the reason for my request. Initially I received no reply. As the days passed and my departure approached I inquired whether my application had at least been examined. "Yes," I was informed. "You may visit Thubten Nyima on Saturday evening at 1900 hours." My old friend's name was no longer Sholkhang Jetrung, nor Wangdü, but Thubten Nyima. At last the moment had arrived: I sat in a Russian jeep with a driver, traveling down to the Kyichu, on whose bank Ngabö, the notorious collaborator, had built himself a small house amidst a garden. This was where Wangdü now lived. Needless to say, my head was in a whirl, and I was looking forward to our encounter with pleasure but also with nervousness. I felt as if I were setting out on some adventure, on some enterprise whose outcome was uncertain. I asked myself if Wangdü for his part was interested in meeting me. Would we find ourselves laughing as in the old days as we sipped our tea? Or would it turn out to be embarrassing? There were no end of questions. I kept telling myself that I could face him with a clear conscience since my views on Tibet's future, which I had explained to him thirty years before, had remained unchanged. For a long time I had been depressed by the news that he had become the Communist Youth leader—until someone had passed on to me his explanation that it was better if a genuine Tibetan looked after the young people than someone whose feelings and thoughts were entirely Chinese.

The car pulled up and I started as if from a dream. So soon. I got out; everywhere was in darkness. I recognized a figure at the yard entrance—Wangdü. He approached and we embraced wordlessly. I was moved; and so, presumably, was Wangdü as he led me to his room in silence, his arm around my shoulders. It was a relatively spacious room, subdivided into two areas, with one large and one small low table. Unfortunately we were not alone; in addition to Drölma, the driver had also sat down at the bigger table. Wangdü and I were seated on a settee, next to each other. I looked at him and felt that I had lost everything that bound us together thirty years previously, even though the memory would always remain.

He had not changed a lot: his hair, admittedly, was a little longer, but I remembered that, even in the old days as a monk-official, he had never had a totally clean-shaven head like the others but had, as a personal gesture perhaps, left a few tufts standing. The same had been true also of his clothes: returning home from the Tsetrung meeting of monk-officials, the first thing he did was to take off his habit and put on a secular Tibetan cloak of the most beautiful light-colored gabardine. Wangdü had always gone his own way, without worrying too much about the demands of the Tibetan hierarchy. In consequence he was demoted by the Regent one day—for "alien body attitude." He had been caught taking photographs with my camera and, while doing so, adopting a crouch undignified for a monk. He was a heavy smoker and invariably was very well-stocked with good English cigarettes, which were forbidden to monks. Snuff was allowed, but Wangdü did not care for it.

After the first few silent and emotionally charged minutes, we burst out laughing at the discovery that we both needed glasses for reading. This broke the spell. I asked about his health because I knew that he had been seriously ill, that he had had tuberculosis and that his teeth were also giving him trouble. Wangdü was eight years younger than I and his narrow, delicately carved face was slightly lined. He seemed to me just as lively and self-assured as in the past, and I asked him if we were still friends. He said we were, and offered me tea with butter, which was a great deal better than the tea we used to drink together in the monasteries. Even so, he apologized that the butter was not quite as fresh as it should be. I asked him if I might have my tape recorder going during our conversation and he replied: "Of course."

His voice sounded serious and thoughtful. I was curious about what he would say to me. He radiated a lot of charm, and after a short while I felt that he had thought a great deal about Tibet's present and future. What he said made sense, and I enjoyed listening to him attentively. Before broaching the delicate subject of politics I wanted to know what he thought about mountaineering and sport—but he urged me to tell him about myself first, about what I had done since leaving Lhasa. In this connection we discovered that, in spite of our close friendship, we had never said good-bye; just before my departure in 1950 he had been sent to Kongpo province on behalf of Ngabö, a cabinet minister. Wangdü had always been a friend of this subsequent collaborator. They used to play mah-jongg and dice together, but there was probably also a common bond between them in their dissatisfaction with monkish rule and their hopes of reforms. But Wangdü had not succeeded in reaching Kongpo, as the Chinese marched into eastern Tibet; instead he had stayed nine months at Gyamda-Dzong. So we had had no opportunity for farewells. I now told him that after my flight from Lhasa I had stayed with the Dalai Lama in the Chumbi valley for three months and had afterward started on my book, *Seven Years in Tibet,* at the Himalaya Hotel in Kalimpong.

I reminded Wangdü of Sanga Chöling, an enchanting spot in the deep forests, surrounded by towering ice-capped mountains; and I also mentioned the 6,000-meter (20,000-foot) Mindrutsari, Lhasa's local mountain, which we had climbed together. Even then he had had no compunction about stepping onto the summit, though it was sacred to the Tibetans as a throne of the gods. Nowadays Wangdü was responsible for the Potala and for organizing trekking.

While we were talking, he lit one cigarette after another, scarcely looking up when his only son, a lively boy of eleven, came in to fill up our cups with tea. Calmly he talked of the time, in 1951, when he returned to Lhasa and for two years worked as a teacher of English and Chinese. He spoke English fairly well, though nowadays, so he said, his command of Chinese was far better. He also remembered the Dalai Lama's return in 1951, when everything remained unchanged and no reforms were carried out. He found life at that time marvelous, for although there was a Chinese representative in Lhasa, everybody could move freely and even go on pilgrimages to India. It was then that Wangdü became Youth Leader. He told me all this, and I interrupted this to say that I had been told about it by Tibetans in India as early as 1956; he had sent word to me, asking me to try to understand why he had taken on the youth job. Now he told me that he had greatly loved the work; knowing that he had always been very fond of dancing, games and sport, I believed him. "Can you still tap-dance?" I asked him. "Of course," he laughed, and we reminisced about how he would call for a board at some cheerful festivity or other and give a tap-dancing display. Even on a bobbing yak-hide boat on the little lake behind the Potala he had once put a board across the gunwales and entertained those present with the sound of his tapping, which was so like some Tibetan national dance rhythms.

While we were talking, his Lhasa Apso came over to me and the conversation turned to dogs. I told him that I had such dogs myself, and that in Lhasa I had seen several strays of this interesting breed— they had been scruffy and unsightly. In the West, Apsos were a precious rarity; they cost a lot of money and were specially bred.

Wangdü returned to the subject of his youth work, told me of his journeys to international youth rallies and observed that he had always come back to Lhasa. There was enthusiasm in his account, and I could see that the job had suited him down to the ground. Then came the cultural revolution and with it the first difficulties. Wangdü spoke of it without any dramatization. He said quite simply: "Those weren't good times." But I knew how bad they had in fact been for him: I had heard reports of his years in prison, that he had been made to run about with the *gyangshing*, a kind of portable wooden pillory, and that, as a "slave-driving noble," he had been subjected to brainwashing and "soul-washing." He admitted: "I did have some difficulties at that time. The Gang of Four was acting without any thought of the consequences. They did great damage to us, to the whole of China. They destroyed everything that was beautiful in the old days. That period is now being called the lost decade of the cultural revolution. Afterward things were a lot better for us. Now we can continue the policies shown us by Mao Tse-tung. If we carry on like that all will be well. All races will be friends, all will have equal rights, no one will use force against another, all will help one another. We are all better off. Six years have passed now, and everything has been steadily improving ever since."

I did not presume to seek the reasons for his attitude. The fact is that he allowed the Chinese to persuade him to become the first Tibetan party member of the "Autonomous Republic of Tibet." The period of the cultural revolution had been terrible for him as well, and he did not like being reminded of it. As for the destruction, he condemned it, and I had the feeling that he fully realized that irreplaceable treasures and records of his culture had been annihilated. He added, however, that Tibetans, too, had taken part in the pillage. I retorted that, as far as I knew, a great number of Tibetans had resisted the wreckers and had suffered greatly for it. But in vain— whatever was of significance to the Tibetans, their monasteries and their temples, an entire religious tradition, had been destroyed. That was roughly how I formulated it to Wangdü, and he nodded his head thoughtfully and repeated: "But the evil Four were sentenced, and everything has taken a turn for the better since."

But I was not so easily diverted and continued to dwell on the losses and the sacrifices of those gallant Tibetans who had saved at least some of their cultural treasures. They dragged books, bronzes and *thangkas* over the Himalayan passes into the free countries of Asia. I told him that some museums, like those in Munich and Zurich, were nowadays in a position to organize exhibitions illustrating the old way of life of Tibet. I did not doubt that my friend had kept his patriotic beliefs but I could not share his views. He continued to talk about Hu Yao-pang, for the past five years the General Secretary of the Communist Party of China, who had paid a one-month visit to Lhasa and whose stay, Wangdü asserted, had been followed by a lot of improvements. He emphasized the exemption from dues for a period of three years, as well as the fact that meat and butter were again on sale in the bazaar. But why, I asked Wangdü, did he not go out into the country himself sometime, where people were starving and living in misery? Without answering my point he went on to speak of road building and canalization, of reconstruction and progress. But did he not see the children performing the heaviest kind of labor so that they too could get a food ration card and did not have to starve to death? Did he not see the compulsory labor, its merciless enforcement? These laborers included learned lamas, nobles, merchants, peasants, old men, children and women. People, in short, whose only crime had been their refusal to bend to the foreign yoke. Did he not see any of this?

There was silence. I was curious to know what his answer would be. Heaven knew what was going on in his head. Wangdü and I clearly differed on Tibet's development. He insisted that, in the past, Tibetan peasants had possessed absolutely nothing, that they had cowered in dark holes, without clothes or food, whereas now they were living in decent housing. Maybe I did not know that. I had to contradict him and point out that I had also been out in the country and had not noticed any such improved housing anywhere. As an official he rarely left the city, and he believed Chinese propaganda. In the region of the Yamdrok Yumtso I had gone into peasant homes, and nothing had changed there since the old days. To my mind this was no loss to the peasants, since clay and wood were pleasant in all seasons and healthier than concrete and tin. At the same time I have no doubt that, when the Chinese started to put up "modern" buildings, the Tibetans were certainly at first impressed by the white concrete and the shiny tin and that they only gradually realized how unstylish, undignified and unhealthy such new housing was.

Wangdü persisted: did I not see that changes were bound to come? Surely we had often discussed the need for them and had been in agreement. "Of course," I concurred, "I remember very well. There had to be changes, but from within and not imposed from outside." I knew that Wangdü had always been courageous; he had been punished and reprimanded by the old government for openly speaking his mind. He had always been in favor of reforms. He remarked: "As they were simply impossible from within, they had to come from outside."

"But tell me, Wangdü, what has really changed?" I questioned him. "You sit in your office and your superior is a Chinese. In the old days it was a senior monk and below him there were the secular officials. The only difference is that previously it was always a Tibetan who was at the top and now it is a Chinese."

Wangdü assured me that during his visit Hu Yao-pang had promised a change in this respect too. Why did I not go and look at the schools? Teaching was again in Tibetan, and that was a further step to future improvements.

I could not help trying to check his optimism by pointing out that the Chinese had proved unreliable and treacherous with regard to the Tibetans in the past. Was it not possible that another Gang of Four would seize power before long? Wangdü rejected this vehemently. He had come to know the Chinese well over the past thirty years, and there could never be another Gang of Four. When I tried to prove to him that Marxism had brought little benefit to the nations over the long period of its existence, either in Poland or in Czechoslovakia or elsewhere, he reacted with surprise: "You call that a long period? When the idea of Marxism has been put into practice for a mere fifty years! Everything is still in its beginnings—but the idea is good."

Wangdü clearly believed what he wanted to believe, he saw only what he wanted to see, and he regarded anyone who thought differently as an opponent. That the idea is good is acknowledged also by others. The Dalai Lama himself has repeatedly pointed to a certain affinity between Buddhism and Marxism, and to real parallels between the two. One need only think of the strict organization of Tibetan monasteries or the religious orders of the Catholic Church.

Wangdü was certainly not one of those who merely talked about the theories of Marxism; he also practiced it. In 1959, when the nobles and the rich were stripped of their estates and lands, Wangdü voluntarily gave up his possessions. Those who had their land expropriated have since been compensated with money, but Wangdü declined compensation. That showed consistency, and was no doubt why he was engaged, as one of few Tibetan officials, in the Restitution Office. The Chinese recognized his qualities and therefore entrusted him with a variety of tasks. I asked him if he remembered what I had said to him in the old days on the subject of native country, nation and homeland. I was uncertain whether to ask him if he still believed in amulets; he once assured me that if, for instance, a talisman came from the Dalai Lama it could protect a person's life even against a rifle bullet. He wanted to prove it to me with a dog, but of course I refused: I did not wish doubts to arise in his mind about his faith. Now he no longer seemed so sure—but I had the impression that he was confusing religion with the old lamaist hierarchy. I did not think that he rejected faith; it was rather that he rejected the old-style government of the people by monks. Both of us agreed that since Hu Yao-pang's visit many more believers dared to pray publicly; this could be observed in particular outside the Tsuglagkhang. In Sera or Drepung, on the other hand, there were only a few pilgrims to be seen.

As Wangdü was also responsible for trekking, I suggested to him that we might realize a long-cherished dream of ours from the old days—to make a journey on foot into the southeast as far as the bend of the Brahmaputra. We had not been able to do this in the past because I had to meet my contractual obligations to the government and he was expected to attend the obligatory daily conferences of the monk-officials. "But now we are free and can afford to indulge our wish," I said. Wangdü hesitated and pointed out that the road into Pemakö province, southeast of the main ridge of the Himalayas, would not be finished for another two years. I said that we would not want to drive or walk along a road but trek through the uniquely beautiful and untouched scenery of southern Tibet. If anyone was able to obtain permission for us, then surely he could. Wangdü replied that this was out of the question because he still had a Chinese official above him. I inquired: "Isn't there some official among your superiors in Peking who would help you get the permit?" At this point Wangdü confessed that he had never set foot in the office and therefore did not know anyone there.

I once more returned to the neutral subject of sport. He told me what a good football team Tibet had, with a place about halfway up the Chinese league. That summer a team from eastern China would come to Lhasa to play them. I proposed that the squad should visit Europe, for matches against our teams, and mentioned that the costs would surely be met. Wangdü reflected for a brief moment and then said that I would have to submit the proposal officially to Peking; in that case, of course, the costs would be met by China.

To me the subject of Tibetan sport also includes the *lung gompa*, those remarkable men who can cover enormous distances in a state of trance, performing that (to us inconceivable) religious and mystical feat at an altitude between 4,000 and 6,000 meters (13,000 to 20,000 feet) without food or drink. These people might be said to be natural competitors for the long-distance running events of the Olympic Games—profane event though this is. It was well-known that the runners from the Kenyan highlands invariably distinguished themselves in such championships. It would be a nice gesture on the part of the Chinese if they allowed the Tibetans to enter as a team in their own right, much as the Russians allow the Mongolians to do; this would at last free them from century-old isolation.

My time with Wangdü passed in a flash, and my driver was getting restless. I could see that I had long exceeded my visiting time. Wangdü smiled at me questioningly; I glanced down at my teacup, which was no longer being replenished, and said good-bye to Wangdü. I hope that, in spite of all our political differences, we shall remain friends.

THE SUFFERINGS OF THE DALAI LAMA'S PHYSICIAN

M y talk with my old friend Wangdü had left a deep impression on me. But as well as my pleasure at having seen him again I was filled with a certain uneasiness about the different way in which we saw Tibet's past and future. Among the many conversations I had had before my visit to Lhasa there had been one with Dr. Tenzing Chödak, the Dalai Lama's physician in Dharamsala, who told me about the miserable time he had spent in Chinese prisons. I am quoting from my interview with the doctor, so that the reader can form his own opinion.

HARRER: "When did you come to India?"

DR. CHÖDAK: "In the tenth month of 1980. When the Dalai Lama's brother, Lobsang Samten, went to Lhasa with his delegation, he requested the Chinese to let me go to India because their mother was seriously ill and wished to be treated by me. As I had been her doctor before, permission was given, though after a year's delay, and I went by truck to Kathmandu through southern Tibet."

HARRER: "You did not flee with the Dalai Lama. Why not?"

DR. CHÖDAK: "In 1959, during the uprising, I had no chance to join the Dalai Lama because my house was at the far end of the city. As the Dalai Lama's physician I was immediately arrested by the Chinese, although I possessed no weapons and was altogether a man of peace. But I had attended the National Assembly a few times, and they were aware of it, and that was evidently their reason for putting me in jail. There were four to five hundred detainees there, mainly nobles and government officials. Some were accommodated twenty to a cell; but there were also cells with ten prisoners, and I was with seven others, and later with only two."

HARRER: "What happened next?"

DR. CHÖDAK: "Although my rank was only that of a *letsempa*, a middle civil servant, I was subjected to brainwashing every day to make me confess to all sorts of things. But only being a medical man I had nothing to confess, and so I had the *gyangshing*, the pillory yoke, put around my neck."

Dr. Chödak then described the size of this wooden device, the way it was fixed with cords, and the two hours that he had to carry the *gyangshing* on his shoulders each day. Although it did not weigh very much, the torture involved the delinquent having to extend his arms like a man crucified, and that was exceedingly painful.

HARRER: "And was that the end of your torture?"

DR. CHÖDAK: "They began to kick me with their boots, and to beat me, after first removing my shirt. When we were twenty to a cell they started group brain- and soul-washing. Everyone was invited to confess his crimes; afterward he would be free to leave the prison. They knew that I had often visited the Dalai Lama at the Norbulingka, but I still had nothing to confess."

HARRER: "Were Tibetans present at these tortures?"

DR. CHÖDAK: "Yes; the Chinese used Tibetan interpreters for the brainwashing."

HARRER: "What happened next?"

DR. CHÖDAK: "They started to throw water in my face until a Chinese doctor came along and told them: 'If you continue treating this man the way you are he'll die in no time.' This colleague, however, did not make that remark from pity but in order to clear himself in case I died. In this way I was maltreated by kicking, beating and with water from the second to the tenth month, that is to say, for eight months. Then we 'incorrigibles' were divided into three groups. I was one of seventy-six Tibetans to be taken to China. We rode on an open truck for twelve days, sleeping in the open, surrounded by Chinese soldiers. At Chuchen we were put into prison, where the food was very scant and we suffered great hardships. There was no tea, no fat, and only 15 *gyama* of flour per month, that's about seven and a half kilograms (sixteen and a half pounds). We were soon like skeletons."

HARRER: "How many survived?"

DR. CHÖDAK: "We were soon so weak we could no longer hold our heads upright, we lost our hair, and were unable to lift our legs. However, we still had our sheepskin coats from Lhasa then; we tore out the wool and ate the leather. One of our fellow prisoners had been a servant in the Dalai Lama's household and possessed a leather belt; he ate it . . . So as not to die of starvation we always had to 'organize' something. We suffered terribly from diarrhea. And some of us screamed continually from pain in the guts. By then, to return to your question, only twenty-one were alive of the seventy-six, and they only managed by sometimes eating the flesh of a dead mule."

HARRER: "How long did matters continue like that?"

DR. CHÖDAK: "Three years. During that time we were made to work in the fields, and would now and again find a bone or some refuse in the manure. My friend Lobsang Gyaltsen once found a stillborn piglet and took one of its bones with him back to the prison. I had warned him that we were very thoroughly searched on returning to our cells in the evening. The bone was in fact discovered, and he was asked why he needed to do such things, seeing that the Chinese were feeding us well. He was led away, and three days later he was dead."

HARRER: "Did you see any Chinese prisoners?"

DR. CHÖDAK: "Yes, and they were very skillful. For instance, they would catch mice and rats. And they would wash out their own excrement and fish out long white worms and eat them."

HARRER: "But one day you were brought back to Tibet?"

DR. CHÖDAK: "Yes, we were taken back to Lhasa in a convoy, just like the outward journey. As we drove over the high passes we had nosebleeds because of the rarefied air, that's how low we were. Finally, they took us to the Trabchi prison in Lhasa."

HARRER: "Did they continue to torture you?"

DR. CHÖDAK: "I was soon transferred to a smaller prison with only about a hundred inmates. Here they once more began their brain- and soul-washing. As his physician, they suggested, I must surely know if the Dalai Lama had had any women. If I confessed to that I would be released immediately. In point of fact, a man I know, the servant of a Rinpoche, had admitted—though it was not true—that his master, who was supposed to be celibate, had had a woman. The man was immediately discharged and commended."

HARRER: "Were you ever taken before a judge?"

DR. CHÖDAK: "Never. Not during the first fourteen years. In fact, I was subjected to perpetual brainwashing in Lhasa for seventeen years altogether. I also had to labor in a quarry for three years, but the physical punishments had ceased. On the twenty-first day of the third month of 1976 I was dispatched as a doctor to a camp called Drigung and was actually allowed home for the weekend. There I worked for three years, until the end of 1978. The food was very much better, and I gradually regained my health. In the autumn of 1980 I was finally allowed to go to India—as I said at the beginning."

Dr. Chödak listed the names of thirteen prisons which had existed then, and estimated the number of detainees in 1978 at 100,000. Subsequently, however, these prisoners had been gradually released.

Finally he told me the following episode that had always stayed with him: "A friend of mine, who was with me in one of the prisons, had smuggled a valuable *khata* into his cell and sewn it into a pillow. One day, when he was detailed to sweep the corridors, he took it out, tied it to his broom and, shouting 'Freedom, freedom' and waving his 'flag,' he stormed down the prison corridors. He was taken away, and I don't know what became of him."

THE CARES OF
THE DALAI LAMA

W hen Lobsang Samten, the Dalai Lama's elder brother, accompanied the delegation to Lhasa in 1979 he also had a very personal mission to fulfill. His mother was seriously ill at the time and had asked her son to inquire of the Chinese if they would allow her to return officially to Lhasa in order to die there. Peking hesitated and instead agreed to the compromise of allowing Dr. Tenzing Chödak, the family physician, to go to India first to attend the sick lady. Unfortunately she was beyond his help: she died in January 1981 and was cremated in a solemn ceremony in Dharamsala.

I have many good memories of this exceptional woman. Just eight days after our arrival in Lhasa, servants called on us with an invitation to the Dalai Lama's house. Aufschnaiter and I were soon standing in front of a huge gate, where we were met, conducted across a large garden with vegetable plots and willow trees to the palace and taken up to the second floor. A curtain was drawn back, there were respectful bows all around, and we were face-to-face with the Lama-king's mother. In a light, spacious room she was sitting on a small throne surrounded by servants—an impressive lady with nobility and dignity. As we presented our white *khatas* a radiant smile spread all over her friendly face. That visit was the beginning of a cordial relationship with that wise and modest woman. We were allowed to participate in numerous festivities in her house, and I remember the official party given on the occasion of the birth of her youngest son, subsequently to be recognized as Ngari Rinpoche, a reincarnation. The party was held only three days after her confinement, yet she cheerfully walked about among the guests as if nothing had happened.

There is no such thing in Tibet as baptism in the Western sense. A child's name, or rather names, are chosen by a lama after he has considered astrological aspects and connections with saints. Eating and drinking goes on for hours. There is nothing disgraceful about being a little tipsy; it is regarded as a contribution to general good humor. Thus ended the day in honor of the little boy whom I now see nearly every year by the side of his brother, the Dalai Lama, in Dharamsala.

Any number of times we would look out from the window of her little summer house in the Norbulingka toward the gate in the yellow wall, where the Regent would emerge after giving lessons to the Dalai Lama. To us this used to be the signal that the Dalai Lama was "free." Two huge, lion-like dogs guarded the normally closed gate in the yellow wall, like Cerberus guarding the netherworld. As the Dalai Lama's mother watched the Regent come out in the mornings, she would whisper to me: "You should go now." Behind the gate was the *chapekhang*. *Chape* is the honorific form for books; the *chapekhang* therefore was the library. From there the Dalai Lama would watch for me expectantly from the window, for the yellow door in the wall to open mysteriously and admit me to the inner palace garden.

The Regent, Tagtra Rinpoche, was a severe and universally feared man. But the Dalai Lama's mother loved her son so much that she sometimes dared to contradict the Regent in his favor. Tagtra Rinpoche is now dead, as is also the older of the Dalai Lama's other two teachers, Trichang Rinpoche, who died in Dharamsala in 1981 at a ripe old age and whose ashes are venerated in a *stupa,* a reliquary shrine. I regularly visited Trichang Rinpoche right up to the time of his death and talked to him about the old days in Lhasa. Unlike the Regent, he had fully understood the Dalai Lama's wish for my company and supported our friendship. The hours the Dalai Lama spent with me were his free time, and these meetings meant a lot to me too. Our time was strictly limited, and just as he received me joyfully so he would anxiously glance at the clock as his free time came to an end. By then his religious instructor would already be waiting for him, punctually, in a pavilion. On one occasion, when I was late, he was already standing by the little window of his palace, looking out for me. His mother received me with a reprimand, as it had not escaped her loving eye that her son had repeatedly glanced at the clock. I was able to give her the reason for my delay and she was reassured that I would never miss an hour with her son irresponsibly.

It was there that, at his brother Lobsang Samten's suggestion, I built a cinema for the Lama-king. I was even officially commissioned by the abbots, and this opened to me all the doors in the inner sanctum of the Norbulingka, doors otherwise closed to everybody. The first film I showed was *Henry V,* starring Laurence Olivier, in which the king soliloquizes on the weight of all the responsibility that falls upon him. And later we read in *Henry IV:* "Uneasy lies the head that wears the crown." I believe that the intelligent boy understood that line even then, and that he surmised what was in store for him. The gods would soon, and still do, lay upon him grievous anxieties about his people and country.

It was many years later, after the horrors of the last few days before their flight in 1959, that I saw the Dalai Lama's mother again in

Dharamsala, where a home had been set up for her in what is called the "Kashmir House." The green roof below her son's residence could be seen gleaming through the trees from a long way off. It was she who first told me about the Chinese atrocities and who related to me with outrage that the streets had been strewn with the magnificently carved covers of the sacred books, and that the golden heads of the gods had been prized out of these bindings with bayonets. Evidently this was too much for the courageous and pious woman; her heart ceased to beat far from her native land.

Thirty years have passed since, yet the Dalai Lama has at no time been able to live without worries, beginning with the invasion of his country in 1951 to the revolt of 1959, when he had to flee. There were stories about the vast quantities of gold the Dalai Lama was supposed to have taken along with him, but I happen to know that this treasure was not that spectacular. The lure of Tibet excites exaggeration about this too.

When I was revisiting Norbulingka in 1982, I endeavored to retrace my steps. I looked for the yellow wall, for the cinema and for the gate to which those dogs with red ruffs were tied with ropes made from white yaks' tails. In the Potrang Sarpa, the new palace built by Pala and Taring Jigme in 1953–4, I met a young Tibetan woman in Chinese dress, a girl who would have been pretty but for her hard features. Her name was Migmar, and she did not strike me as a good representative of Tibet; she merely intensified the nostalgia with which I was seeking those old familiar spots—the cinema, the Dalai Lama's house and that of his parents. Everything was desolate and locked up. We had planted a garden with marvelous flowers all around; now nothing bloomed, everything was barren, and the pools were dry. I walked through the Potrang Sarpa, gazed at the frescoes of Tibet's history, and inwardly felt sorry for Migmar, who evidently knew all too little of these things.

15

"No Place
Like Home"

The first thing that struck me when I visited the places where I had formerly lived in Lhasa was the absence of flowers. Tibetans love colorful blossoms, and wherever they had an old container—a cooking pot or some chipped porcelain—they would plant flowers in it. I was, as usual, accompanied by my Chinese chaperon, who had volunteered to help me find the Tsarong house, where I had been received after my arrival in Lhasa. I had some difficulty finding my way, even though I had with me the old city plan I had drawn with Aufschnaiter. Everything was so built up that I had to ask people in the street. Eventually, after a long search, I found an old Tibetan who said: "I know where you used to live." He led me through a narrow little street, which was just as dirty as it had been in my time, and said: "This is my house, come in." He steered us into a tiny courtyard, put a ladder made from two tree trunks lashed together against the wall, and I climbed up with him onto a flat roof. And indeed, right there at my feet was the big Tsarong house and, to the right of it, separated by a wall, were the quarters where I had lived for so long. The old Tibetan was trying to do me a favor; without any embarrassment he drew up his ladder and lowered it into the courtyard of the Tsarong house. I only just managed to stop him. I knew that Chinese officers were now accommodated there.

I quickly took a few photographs and instantly a Chinese emerged and gestured that this was forbidden. Here, too, there was not a single flower or shrub. In vain did I look for the trees I had planted. The first fountain in a Tibetan garden, which I had installed, had also disappeared. (The very first fountain in Tibet had been built by George Sherriff in 1944 in the garden of the British Representative.)

I nevertheless wanted to inspect the building at close quarters, to discover exactly what had survived and what had vanished. We descended to the little courtyard to the right of Tsarong's house and reached my old quarters. Because of the serious shortage of accommodation and the need for people to content themselves with less, my apartment had been subdivided. My fine window had had a door fitted along its right half because that room was now occupied by an entire family. I used to have a second room in the old days, as well as a kitchen. Now there was a passage between the two apartments, and in the passage a big tree. I remembered planting it as a small willow sapling. The house was inhabited by two pleasant families, and when I talked to one of the women she obligingly let me see my old rooms. There, for the first time, I had a sense of time having stood still. The place was still furnished in exactly the same way, except that my table had been higher and had stood up against the window to give me more light for drawing my maps for the government. A new feature was the electric meter; my lighting then had been with oil and tapers. The two families had flowers in the window, planted in much-loved disused Tibetan pots. For a long time no one had dared to keep flowers, remembering how the Red Guards had smashed their flowerpots to make sure nothing cheerful or colorful remained in Tibetan homes.

I also visited Yütok's former house, where I had stayed for a couple of years while that famous noble was traveling in India. He had requested me to plant flowers and vegetables in his garden during his absence and had left me all his servants to command. The house was near the famous Turquoise Bridge, the Yütok Sampa. This magnificent bridge, roofed over with turquoise ceramic tiles, has since been surrounded by a wall and now only serves as a toolshed; in the old days one used to ride across a little stream under its roof. Here, exactly opposite, should have been Yütok's house—but it had burned down and only the bare walls and charred window openings were left. No one could explain to me what had happened. Confidentially, in whispers, it was said that the house had probably been set on fire by the Tibetan underground movement, as had the big registry office in the Chinese quarter, which had housed the occupying power's records on Tibetan families. This explanation may well be correct, as some official red boards with Chinese writing were still standing in front of the building.

I was unable to find the house of Foreign Minister Surkhang, whose son I had saved from drowning. After that incident he, too, had placed his fine house at my disposal—a beautiful big building near the river, and called Polingka. There, in his splendid garden, I had also planted vegetables; indeed my servant Nyima, who accompanied me on my flight as far as the Brahmaputra and then returned to Lhasa, lived on these vegetables for the period immediately after the Chinese invasion and by selling them earned his keep. Naturally, during my present visit to Lhasa, all the people I had lived with thirty years before came back to my mind. Top of the list, needless to say, was Peter Aufschnaiter, my experienced companion, my senior by thirteen years, whose motto *"Esse quam videri"*—to be rather than to seem—had also always been my guideline. When he, like myself, had to leave Lhasa he decided to make for Nepal via Kyirong. He was determined to see once more that village of "blissful happiness," where we had spent several months after escaping from our internment camp. I myself traveled with the Dalai Lama's party to the Chumbi valley, and on into Sikkim. Because I was going straight to India I had taken Peter Aufschnaiter's valuable archaeological finds, made during his excavation of a canal in Lhasa, with me across the Himalayas and into India. Unfortunately the items have not so far arrived in Switzerland, where his excavation notes are kept and are already being studied by Martin Brauen at the Ethnographical Museum in Zurich.

Hugh Richardson, the British representative in Lhasa, had some trouble with Aufschnaiter and me. He had to remind the Tibetan government of the request by the Indian government that we should be returned to India. They asked whether the Indian government would not wait for some time and, when he saw that we were doing work of value to the Tibetans and were entirely apolitical and that we had been brought to Tibet by totally different interests, the matter was quietly dropped. We got to know each other better, played tennis together, and sometimes bridge, and were asked to his home. I was able to borrow English books from him, as well as the films which I subsequently showed to the Dalai Lama at the cinema I had built. Even after India's declaration of independence in 1947, Richardson stayed in Lhasa until 1950. Nowadays he is one of the greatest experts on Tibet's past and the author of a Tibetan dictionary and grammar. He has also written an excellent book on Tibetan history and a detailed description of the *doring,* those carved stone pillars on which historical events are recorded. Later he taught as a visiting professor at various universities, the longest period in Seattle. Richardson now lives in St. Andrews, where he is a member of the world's oldest golf club and where, thanks to him, I am a member too. Whenever I am in Scotland I enjoy a round of golf with him.

Two other Britons in Lhasa were Reginald Fox and Robert Ford, whose fate was also affected by India's independence. When the Chinese were threatening Tibet the Tibetan government took Fox over as a radio engineer; he was instructed to set up transmitters at a number of strategically important spots. For his work in Chamdo, the capital of Kham province and the focus of the conflict, Fox recruited the young Englishman Robert Ford as an assistant. Ford traveled to Chamdo with a big caravan and soon it was possible to talk to him by radio telephone. Unfortunately the notes Ford had made of these harmless conversations were to be his downfall a short while later. The Chinese made the most incredible accusations against him and jailed him in Chungking for five years. His book *Captured in Tibet* (Harrap, 1952) records his experiences. Later he became a British consul-general and, thanks to his command of numerous languages, there were few countries in the world where he could not have been posted. He retired in 1983. I am still in touch with him. Reginald Fox married a Tibetan girl named Nyima from the Chumbi valley and later died in Kalimpong.

Two most interesting visitors arrived in Lhasa in 1949—the Americans Lowell Thomas Senior and Junior. The two filmed and photographed the country and its people. The son displayed great journalistic skill in writing a best-seller, and the father, a well-known radio commentator in the United States, made tape recordings for his programs. I made friends with the father, and it was he who sent me the first card from Lhasa in 1978. He was one of the people around Arthur Schlesinger—one of the first men whom the Chinese allowed to come to Lhasa as President Kennedy's special adviser. Thomas reported dejectedly about the changes in Lhasa: "You wouldn't recognize Lhasa. Mao banners everywhere and Mao songs blaring from top of the Potala." Thomas was president of the Explorer Club in New York, and we used to meet at some of its annual dinners. Mentally active to the end, and with contacts all over the world, he died recently, aged nearly ninety.

There is no doubt that my stay in Tibet left its stamp on me for the rest of my life. I did not resume my former occupation as geography and sports teacher but instead took up again what I had begun in my youth: climbing and exploration of unknown regions. These enterprises had always been pervaded by a particular love of Asia and, subsequently, more especially the Tibetan cultural sphere. To this day travel is the great fulfillment of my life—but as I am getting older I regard it as the privilege of age to be interested more in journeying toward and around the mountains, and meeting people, plants and animals, then conquering their summits. The element of adventure seems to have dwindled a little, but it gives me no less happiness than before.

I should not wish to conclude this chapter without relating an amusing incident involving another old acquaintance. When I was in England in 1953 to attend the launching of *Seven Years in Tibet*, translated into English, and with a preface by Peter Fleming, I also gave a number of lectures. Just before a talk at the Royal Festival Hall, I received a letter from Colonel Williams, my former camp commandant at Dehra Dun. He said: "As the CO of your prisoners' camp in India I had to take the blame for your successful escape; today, to add insult to injury, I even had to pay for a ticket to listen to how you did it." It is typical of the fairness and sense of humor of the British that a storm of applause greeted my reading of this letter in the packed hall.

16

TODAY AND
YESTERDAY

It was an ordinary day in April 1982. Not the New Year, nor even the fourth month, in which Buddha was born and died, and which therefore was a month of fasting and celebration. Even so, I saw more pilgrims on Barkhor than at the time of the great feasts in the old days. They walked around the sacred temple, flung themselves down and made their way forward by measuring the length and sometimes the breadth of their bodies on the ground; others were turning prayer wheels. Some of them were carrying not the usual knobs of butter offered up to the gods but small flasks of oil, as well as the beautiful old *tsamku*, small leather pouches containing roast barley flour, the famous *tsampa*. At every altar I saw again the small heaps of *tsampa*, usually carried away by an old monk who also poured the oil into the butter lamps. Offerings were so plentiful that the lamps were overflowing and there was scarcely room for any more heaps of *tsampa*. This surplus represents the food of the temple guardian and of the few monks who nowadays act as temple guardians. But these men's rations were but a small portion of the offerings; the bulk was filled into canisters to be delivered to the temple administration. I also saw banknotes on the altars, though now only Chinese money.

Our tourist group from Europe and America had so-called "tourist money," which could be used only for purchases in the department stores set up specially for visitors. This, of course, is a government measure designed to control foreign currency. Everywhere now one saw only Chinese paper money, and I often recalled the pretty silver coins with the eight lucky symbols in use during my time in Lhasa. These are now sometimes offered as souvenirs in the bazaar, and on one occasion an elderly Tibetan woman who knew me from the past furtively slipped one of these *tranka* into my pocket as a rarity.

Since the recent tax reductions, the traditional knobs of butter have again appeared in the market, a little fresher than in the old days because transport is faster. There was also Chinese tea—but I never once saw the sweet tea which used to be popular in Lhasa, nor the often-described butter tea. In our Guest House we were served exclusively Chinese food of mediocre quality. I never even saw *momo* or *sha-bagle,* both Tibetan delicacies of highly spiced pastry filled with meat. The evening meal had to be taken punctually at 6:30 P.M.; the waitresses were young Tibetans employed by the Guest House. If one happened to be late, or wanted another helping, one was told that the cook had left at 7 P.M. How different from the old days! Cooks and servants used to love their masters and would have gladly got out of bed at midnight to prepare a meal. I was thinking of my servant Nyima, who had looked after me in Lhasa for many years and who had been greatly devoted to me. Time and again he would wait for me late at night at the door of some host or other of mine, even though I had expressly told him to go home. He feared lest I should be attacked on the way home and was ready with his sword to protect me with his own life. Nothing at all to do with slavery, as the Chinese were fond of asserting—indeed, the very opposite.

Inside their small houses the Tibetans, of course, still cook their traditional dishes with barley flour and sun-dried yak meat, and they also make their delicious *momo*. The same is true of their dress. Back in Szechwan I had first observed that only very few people of the Shan race were seen wearing their magnificent costumes among the green-and-blue-clad "ants." These minorities from the Burmese frontier were nervous and shy; everybody looked at them and wanted to take photographs because they were such a rare and pretty sight. Tibetans have not yet reached that stage. They are more reserved and still hesitate to put on their best clothes after years of strict prohibition on deviating from the standard look of the Chinese. No colorful embroidered clothes, no jewelry—everybody was to look alike, with no distinction between nobles, citizens and monks. In my opinion, the Tibetans should again be encouraged to wear the colorful traditional clothes before it is too late and future generations will only be able to see them in museums.

While strolling in the bazaar I was delighted to find that the Tibetan merchants were still using the ancient Chinese abacus, that simple calculator of wooden beads which had so often, in the old days, made me look foolish. At the request of some Tibetans I had also taught them arithmetic, e.g., multiplication and addition. And while I was still writing, the abacus had long "spewed out" the answer. It is quite simply like a modern calculator: you put in a figure, then another, and the result is there, automatically, to be read off. Incidentally, there is another difference in their method of calculating—the Chinese and Tibetans, unlike ourselves, when giving you change, first give you the large units and then the small ones.

I should also like to say a few words about their totally different concept of time, as I had observed it over many years of living among them and as I have since succeeded in adopting it myself. More than ever before, people in our hectic age are dreaming of imperturbability, tranquillity and harmony, and are hoping to attain these through mysticism and meditation. But I believe we can only dream of it—we can never achieve that state. It is too deeply rooted to be simply transplanted into Western culture; it is a spring which we must discover for ourselves. One has to be an Asian, to have grown up in that environment, in order to practice yoga genuinely—for us it will always only be a gymnastic exercise without spiritual effect.

Several interesting episodes from my life among the Tibetans clearly illustrate their totally different concept of time. To start with, no one in the country, except a few progressive Tibetans, possessed clocks in the old days. And yet they could very accurately name the hour when, for instance, they wanted to meet. There was *chake tangpo,* the first crowing of the cock, followed shortly by the second and third; then came *namlang,* first light; next came *nyimashar,* sunrise, and so on. In this way the twenty-four hours were divided into short spans of time.

One of my duties in Lhasa had been to pass on to the Dalai Lama and to the Foreign Ministry all news from the outside world, as I heard it on my battery radio. One day—it must have been in 1948 or 1949—I brought the Dalai Lama and his ministers a piece of news that was sensational to me: a jet-propelled aircraft had crossed the Atlantic in a mere six and a half hours. I told them this, full of enthusiasm, and was looking at them expectantly—but there was only an embarrassed silence until one of the ministers broke it by asking: "Why?" I had no answer.

Much the same happened to my wife when we were entertaining a Tibetan lama friend at our home in Europe. It was a winter evening, toward 10 P.M., when the Tibetan suddenly rose to go to the station. "What time is your train, then?" we asked. "I don't know," he replied. "Why don't you let me look it up for you?" I said. "No," he replied, "there's no need. I'll go to the station and there's bound to be a train sometime."

It is with similar imperturbability that the Tibetans view the transformations in their country. When, following Hu Yao-pang's visit and one-month stay in Tibet, conditions did in fact begin to improve because a number of Chinese had been replaced in the administration by native officials, the Tibetans at first adopted a wait-and-see attitude. Today they know that, by way of exchange, the Chinese have sent more troops into the country, so that the over-all number of Chinese has remained unchanged. As they were saying in Lhasa: "The blue Chinese are leaving but the yellow ones are taking their place." Soldiers instead of civilians. And yet—the no-mads are no longer ordered to settle down and are once more free to roam as in the old days. The lowering of the taxes immediately gave rise to a free market. So what happened? Cautiously at first and in small quantities, knobs of butter sewn into animal stomachs and bladders were offered for sale in the bazaar. A silver lining on the horizon, or more *dʒüma*, as the Tibetans call it? No real freedom, since Peking continues strictly to control the country.

Most Chinese soldiers and officials lack the intelligence and far-sightedness of Hu Yao-pang. They fail to see the value of the Ti-betan people underneath the poverty and the squalor; they do not feel at ease in Tibet. The government tackled the problem by in-creasing their pay and promising to fly them home for leave. Only in this way was it possible to send Chinese officials and troops, at least for a short term of duty, into that "unsocialist" region. Nobody wished to go voluntarily to that inhospitable land with its sandstorms and bitterly cold winter nights. How much better to stay at home in Szechwan province with its warm tropical climate, with its forests and its civilization of automobiles and cinemas. But this attitude of the ordinary Chinese had one advantage: wherever I walked around and asked, in army camps and hutments, I found civilian work such as administration and catering was already being done by Tibetans. So there is a glimmer of hope here too.

Alongside the example of Bhutan, which I mentioned in an earlier chapter, I also can envisage a Chinese community on the lines of the European community. Why should it not be possible for that vast Chinese country to live peacefully in unison with its minorities? The Chinese flag with its five stars, one of which stands for Tibet, actually suggests such an approach. Prerequisites do not seem to be all that unpromising, and there is no doubt about Chinese efficiency, long acknowledged by the outside world. Tibet and the other minorities—allowed to keep their language, culture, customs and traditions—might each simply be a part of that enormous yellow state provided it was emphasized that they were not minorities but partners. Decisive for Tibet, of course, is the opinion of the Dalai Lama. Here, then, is an opportunity for submitting to the Chinese a well-thought-out scheme, in which the Lama-king would unmistakably and realistically set out his conditions. On returning from Lhasa my first steps led me to Dharamsala to report my impressions to the Dalai Lama.

17

I REPORT TO
THE DALAI LAMA

It seems important to me to acquaint the reader, even at this point halfway through the book, with the remarks and ideas expressed to me by the Dalai Lama when I called on him in Dharamsala after my trip to Tibet.

I had inwardly digested my impressions and was now standing before his house, about to report to him on his country, which he had not seen for twenty-four years. Summoned in, I entered and presented to him a *khata* and several videotapes about Tibet. I said to him: "I have known you for nearly forty years but each time we meet my heart pounds as on that day in Lhasa when I saw you for the first time." He burst out laughing merrily, in his cheerful way. I introduced my grandchildren to him, and Irene, the elder of the two girls, handed him a *Sachertorte* from Vienna. I warned him to find out first whether this present we had brought all the way to northern India, over a distance of some 6,000 miles and in the heat, had not turned into a sticky mess. This made him laugh again because I called the sticky mess *thugpa,* a kind of thick soup that is a great favorite in

Lhasa's Western Gate is now totally destroyed.

The Dalai Lama's mother on the roof of her palace.

Opposite: Peter Aufschnaiter with Tsarong's daughter.

Ngari Rinpoche as a child.

Harrer, Wangdü, Mr Bessac, Lobsang Samten and Surkhang Wangchuk.

Hugh Richardson, the British representative in Lhasa.

A group of Tibetan dignitaries inspecting the dam I had built with Peter Aufschnaiter in 1949 (when this picture was taken). Nobody believed the dam would stand up – but when I returned in 1982 it was still intact.

Monk police on the roof of the central temple in Lhasa.

Samye, in the Brahmaputra valley, Tibet's oldest monastery, is now totally destroyed.

The Dalai Lama's last examination at the monastery of Ganden shortly before his departure.

The fleeing Dalai Lama's caravan passing the fortress of Gyantse.
The lines of stones along the road are designed to prevent evil spirits from
crossing his escape route.

In 1951 the young Dalai Lama was carried in a litter over the Himalayan
passes to his first place of exile in the Chumbi valley.

The impressive fortress of Shigatse towered above Tibet's second biggest town. This picture was taken before the Chinese destroyed the building.

Tibet. But even if it had all turned into *thugpa,* we hoped he would appreciate our good intentions.

The Dalai Lama asked by what route I had gone to Tibet, and I explained that I had taken a plane from Chengdu to Lhasa. "On our approach, in the Brahmaputra valley, the first terrible sight we saw confirmed all the bad news about Tibet's oldest monastery, Samye; it is totally destroyed. One can still make out the outer wall, but none of the temples or *stupas* survives."

The Dalai Lama asked if there had been any restrictions on taking photographs, and I told him that it was not as in Russia or in some other countries. "There was no ban of any kind. We were allowed to take pictures at all railway stations, bridges and also from the air." I related that I had met Drölma, who was now a tourist guide, and that her Chinese colleagues had warned me against talking to her. I told the Dalai Lama that a Chinese guide had continually asked me why on earth we wanted to spend a lot of money to visit such a backward country.

The Dalai Lama wanted to know how the Tibetans had reacted to me—the ordinary people in the city and the peasants in the countryside. I told him that on Barkhor there were more pilgrims prostrating themselves now than ever before, that most of them came from Amdo province, but that there were also many Khampas, as proud as ever. "With heads held high they walk through the streets of Lhasa and they enjoy the same respect as in the past. The people from Amdo have a six-day journey on an open truck and it costs them a small fortune. There were a great many pilgrims prostrating themselves: in the paved area in front of the Tsuglagkhang gate some twenty or more were flinging themselves on the ground. Incidentally, there are hardly any Tibetans in the Chinese quarter, and conversely very few soldiers are seen on Barkhor."

I had brought along for him some photographs showing believers and other scenes, and I described the hideous view one had from the Potala now of tin roofs and hutments. The Dalai Lama looked at the photographs for a long time and then said: "These are all shoddy buildings which will not last." I answered: "Of course, they are not as strongly built as Tibetan houses and provide no protection against the cold."

There were two television men in my party, and I introduced them to the Dalai Lama. They had brought him a few films, so he could get an idea of the way we were planning our report on Tibet.

The conversation then turned to details of our trip. Wangdü's name was mentioned. I said: "I believe that at heart he is as Tibetan as ever. He merely confuses religion with the Church, and ecclesiastical institutions with faith."

The decision on the Dalai Lama's flight had been made not on personal grounds but for reasons of state policy. The question then cropped up of whether it had been right for him to leave his country, or if he would have done better to stay there. I inquired if he himself was considering returning. He replied: "The purpose of my stay abroad is to serve my people. The matter is basically very simple: if the people in Tibet are really happy then the exiles and I will return home. However, until that situation is achieved I am convinced that I can be of more use to my country outside its frontiers. What do you think of this view?"

I tried to find an answer: "I share your opinion. The moment you return you are in Chinese lands. And we know how untrustworthy they are. Just think of what happened to the Panchen Lama, with his nineteen years of house arrest. On the other hand, as long as you live outside Tibet you are a great worry to them. The Chinese have meanwhile come to understand that wherever you are there also is the heart of the Tibetan people. Of course, one has got to consider a future return. What are your feelings about this?"

The Dalai Lama answered: "At present a lot of things are getting better in Tibet, and I have a great admiration for the present Chinese leadership. It is showing great courage in admitting to mistakes in the past. And it has promised to treat us a little more gently. In principle I am very optimistic and hopeful. But although some things have improved, we are a long way from being satisfied. But I believe that a positive development is taking place. That makes it more difficult for me to say when I shall return. I receive many letters, and I also gather from conversations that it is widely held that I should not on any account return just yet. Nearly all of Tibet's foreign friends—and that includes you—similarly keep emphasizing that it would be unwise to return at this moment."

Full of outrage, I reported to him about UNESCO's international conference on cultural policy in Mexico City, which had just come to an end after three weeks' discussions. More than two hundred resolutions had been adopted there. The final declaration, unanimously adopted, had emphasized the need to preserve the cultural identity of all nations and to recognize the equality and dignity of all cultures. Freedom of thought and speech were indispensable. "Is it not ironic," I asked the Dalai Lama, "that millions are spent on such conferences and on passing resolutions which are a downright mockery of everything that is happening in Tibet and in other countries?"

I asked him about his contacts with the Peking government. He said: "I have been negotiating with the Chinese for years. I have sent delegations to Tibet to find out what things are like there. I now have direct contact with the government. My relations with Peking have undoubtedly become better and more open. I must now wait and see if their good intentions are translated into deeds. Unfortunately there is a wide gulf between the intentions of the government in Peking and those Chinese who implement its instructions in Lhasa. Nevertheless, I believe that things are moving. But it will take time."

"When you mention time it should be borne in mind that you

people in Asia think in totally different time concepts from us in Europe. Nevertheless, I too can see a silver lining. Did your latest delegates bring back anything positive from Peking?"

"I am convinced that the present Peking government is negotiating seriously and honestly. It is much more humane than the previous one. When Hu Yao-pang, the present Chinese leader, was in Lhasa he publicly admitted the errors committed by the government in the past. He also apologized for their frightful actions. Tibet has a great cultural heritage to preserve, and it is that which gives a meaning to the people's lives and gives them courage to face their existence. That is why it is important for us to concern ourselves with Tibetan culture and religion; even in exile we have done everything in our power to preserve them. I have traveled a great deal over the past twenty-four years: I have been to North America, Europe, Australia and Japan. We have set up a great many new Buddhist centers and, by participating in major exhibitions, have acquainted the world with our culture."

I assured him that the free world could not possibly have a better ambassador for the cause of peace than His Holiness. I hoped he would understand that I was proud and happy to have been his friend for more than thirty years. On parting I assured the Dalai Lama that, even though his people may have lost all their material wealth, no one could take from them their spiritual values. I would regard it as my duty to arouse sympathy and understanding, also with my new book, and to ensure by means of lectures, exhibitions, conversations and pictures that Tibetan culture would continue to live on.

18

"OUR CULTURE IS OUR STRONGEST WEAPON"

While in Dharamsala I also had an opportunity to hear the views of leading Tibetans on their country's present and future. My first conversation was with Ngari Rinpoche, the Dalai Lama's youngest brother, who is now permanently at his brother's side as his private secretary.

"China's occupation of Tibet was the most frightful kind of colonization the world has ever seen," Ngari Rinpoche said. "In point of fact, the maltreatment of Tibetans, the brainwashing procedures and the famines started long before the Gang of Four with its Red Guards tried to destroy the country totally. Truth is on the side of the Dalai Lama and the Tibetans in exile. And it is encouraging that they feel they are on the right road. Now, after twenty-three years, everyone agrees that the Tibetans were right. I regard the 'thaw' as a positive factor and the various improvements as a glimmer of hope. But the Chinese must treat the Tibetans with more human respect. China is a vast country with a great tradition and remarkable cultural values. The two nations must coexist—but not under the system applied by the Chinese in the past. The changes are encouraging—but only the future will show whether the Chinese are serious about them."

Ngari Rinpoche continued: "I personally believe that the government in Peking really intends to change its attitude. But implementation of Peking's instructions by the authorities within the country or by their Tibetan collaborators is another matter. There is in fact a vast difference between the Peking government and the people actually in power in Lhasa.

"The collaborators, the *go nyipa* or 'two-headed ones,' are the worst types Tibet has produced. Only the lickspittles survive among the Chinese and are employed by them. These 'two-headed' Tibetans have no sense of morality. The majority of Tibet's intelligentsia either fled the country or perished. The collaborators are opportunists anxious to save their own skins. I cannot even blame men like Ngabö, Wangdü or Kapshö—when violence is used, what else can they do but collaborate? At heart they are honest Tibetans.

"We who are close to the Dalai Lama believe that a more global view should be taken of the situation, at least within a general Asian context. And the worldwide conflicts are a lot more important: America must cooperate with China and Pakistan; Indira Gandhi, in consequence, is compelled to make deals with the Soviets. An ideal permanent solution agreed among the Big Three—China, Russia and India—would be a Tibetan buffer state that would guarantee peace for a long time to come. As once before!

"The Chinese are unlikely ever to give up Tibet. But history has shown that every so often rebellions break out, so the possibility cannot entirely be ruled out in the future. Besides, we Tibetans have time. China will find itself in increasing difficulties, as no less than sixty percent of the country is made up of provinces with minorities, such as Sinkiang, Manchuria, Mongolia and Tibet."

I concurred with Ngari Rinpoche and pointed out that the Tibetans could afford to think in terms of generations, in decades and in centuries. They possess a great culture, a 1,000-year-old history of medical learning and deeply rooted scholarship. They had proved to the world that even in exile they were a nation and therefore were entitled to be regarded as an independent state. Perhaps they would eventually convince world opinion of this fact. Ngari Rinpoche retorted: "If only the USA were to say, 'The Tibetans are an independent nation. Unless the Chinese allow them their independence we shall impose sanctions and stop our subsidies.'"

But all that needs time. The only realistic aspect of all these ideas about the future is that the Tibetans have that time. The Chinese urgently need foreign assistance, for instance with hard currency; if therefore the great countries were to support the Tibetans I believe that sanctions could be one way to obtain freedom for them. Of course, the Tibetans realize that to support countries like China is a good business proposition for these great nations. After all, China is the country with the largest population in the world and hence is an ideal market.

In the Dalai Lama the Tibetans have a remarkable ambassador, a man with charisma, who travels, and has to travel, around the world in order to champion their rights everywhere. The Chinese committed a great blunder in trying to wipe out Tibetan culture. They failed to understand that Tibet is an ethical unity, united under the Dalai Lama and their religion. The Tibetan youth organization has repeatedly demanded the return of liberty by force. Once modeling themselves on Arafat and the Palestinians, they have since realized that this is not the right way. Nevertheless it is good to know that there are young people who are prepared to sacrifice their time to an idea. Of course, in their hearts the Tibetans know that they may have to fight and risk their lives. But one has to be realistic. They have no weapons and must resort to other means. Again and again the Rinpoche repeated: "We have our culture. That is our best weapon. That is why we must cultivate and develop still further our religion, philosophy and medicine. They are the key to the Tibet of the future. In any case, culture is the greatest power on earth. The best illustration of this is Iran. The United States, with all its money, was powerless against Ayatollah Khomeini's religion. Or think of the great influence of the Pope in the Catholic world."

Jigme Tsarong, who had been involved in Tibetan medicine for many years, similarly told me: "Culture is a peaceful force, and the Chinese must understand that we Tibetans are strong through our moral beliefs and our religion, and that no brute force can ever change that. That is also why our medicine is so successful—because it is a combination of spirit and matter. You Westerners treat only what you can actually see. We with our spiritual medicine also get a grip on the invisible. We know that a spiritual approach is invariably superior. They can torture and martyr us, but they can never change the spirit that way."

It is their awareness of freedom that enables Tibetans to think thus. It took the Chinese thirty years to understand this wisdom of the Tibetans, and maybe that is why they have now changed to a softer tune. But who can tell if this is not again just a matter of tactics, designed to encourage the people by tolerance in order to switch to a new hard line later. Whatever the Chinese are doing for the Tibetans now, they are not above suspicion of one day doing just the opposite.

19

FRANK WORDS FROM
LOBSANG SAMTEN

Lobsang Samten, the Dalai Lama's elder brother, was not quite as conciliatory as Ngari Rinpoche, whose words reflected the Dalai Lama's way of thinking. He had been a member of the delegation of the Dalai Lama that had visited Tibet from August to November 1979. The events of that time defy description: religion and patriotism entered into an alliance against which the Chinese were powerless.

One must sympathize with Lobsang Samten's words, with their impotent fury and boundless sadness. At their very first stop in Peking they had been met by a senior Chinese official with the words: "What a people you are, you Tibetans! In spite of all the force we used we have achieved nothing. We brainwashed you, we tortured and killed you, but nothing broke your faith." This is entirely in line with what I was told by a German geologist who had attended some conference in Peking. When the fate of Tibet was mentioned, a high official had to admit that they now realized that nothing could be done there without religion. Lobsang Samten experienced this in an impressive manner on his visit to Tibet. He was mobbed by thousands of believers who welcomed him with tears; he was in fact the ideal messenger for his brother: cheerful, warm-hearted and very accessible. He played with the children, he picked up a scythe and worked with the peasants in the fields. No one would have expected that kind of thing from a brother of the Dalai Lama. For a while the people were happy again.

But Lobsang was also outraged: "Over the past thirty years the Chinese have stripped the Tibetans of everything, and now they are beginning to grant them a few liberties. They are saying: 'Come on, then, show us how prosperous you can become if you're given your own way.' But how can we achieve anything when they have taken everything from us?"

Lobsang had noticed, just as I did later, that the houses and rooms inhabited by Tibetans were miserable and cold. Clean, certainly, but devoid of all ornaments: there were no *thangkas,* no bronzes and no altars. Yet these objects used to be found in every household. Although since 1979 they have again been permitted, they quite simply no longer exist because they have been stolen or destroyed. The Tibetans manage with pictures of the Dalai Lama; in 1979, when Lobsang Samten was in Lhasa, these were still rarities. But in 1982 I was able to observe that in some temples such pictures were again found, publicly, on the altars. Lobsang's comment was: "The Chinese sent experts on Tibetan culture into the monasteries to round up, first of all, all the valuable items, especially all gold objects. Then came the Red Guards and finally the looters. At Ganden there had been whole convoys, carrying off loot by the truckload. No one is quite sure where these treasures were taken—but certainly to China. After that the Tibetans were forced in at gunpoint, and incited: 'You can go in now, all this is yours anyway. That's what the nobles and lamas took from you in the past, now it's yours to take!'"

Lobsang had seen butter and meat in the market at Shigatse, but when he subsequently spoke secretly to Tibetans they admitted that it would all be collected and carted away again that evening—the display had been solely for his and the tourists' benefit.

Lobsang spent altogether sixteen days in Lhasa in September and October, and after that had visited his native Amdo. There he was told that there had been such ghastly famine that people had eaten dogs and even human corpses. Another story from Amdo was reported by Thubten Jigme Norbu, the Dalai Lama's eldest brother. He had passed slaughterhouses in the Chang-thang, north of Lhasa, where numerous nomads lived with their herds. Every day huge numbers of yaks and horses were slaughtered there and taken by refrigerated truck to Langchow and thence by air to Hong Kong. Norbu said: "At home there is famine, and on the menu of Hong Kong hotels I have myself seen Tibetan yak steaks, sold by the Chinese for precious foreign currency."

When I asked what was being offered in Tibetan beer shops and restaurants, Lobsang merely laughed. They were all under Chinese management, belonged to the government, and in order to eat there one needed food ration cards, just as in China. When he asked for it, Lobsang had actually received some *chang*, Tibetan beer, but this had been specially made for him. He told me that at Gyangtse there had been some forty people in a bar, including a few Chinese. He invited them all to have a drink; he thought the Tibetan beer was excellent. Then a Tibetan made him taste the *chang* that had been served to the rest of the guests, and that was dreadful . . .

In reply to my question about how it was that prayer flags could be seen on the top of Chagpori but tourists were not allowed up, Lobsang Samten said: "Strangers are kept away from anywhere where they might see destruction at close quarters; that's why Ganden is out of bounds too. At Drepung, for instance, a few façades which are visible from the road below have been restored, but behind them are ruins." Lobsang confirmed that ninety-nine percent of all Tibetan monasteries had been destroyed, including the magnificent rock-face monastery of Kyetsang, just outside Lhasa, and the huge Kundeling west of Potala, as well as all the hermitages above Sera and Drepung. When I observed to Lobsang that in the spring of 1982, during my visit, work had been going on on the lions outside the Gyangtse temple, he said to me: "I swear to you, Henrig, that when I was there in 1979, a man was working with a spatula on that same lion. Doesn't this prove it—it's all *dʒüma*, all eyewash!"

When I asked where the photograph had been taken from that showed a room with a huge number of wrecked figures, gold foil from gargoyles and other ornaments, he told me the following story: When his delegation was visiting the Norbulingka the Chinese had stopped controlling the Dalai Lama's delegates; they roamed at will. And when they insisted on seeing the rooms in the Dalai Lama's old temper the doors were unlocked for them. Lobsang: "And before us were those mountains of gold from our temples! But everything was broken and battered, and when they saw our horrified faces the Chinese asked what on earth we wanted to keep that 'rubbish' for."

Thus the Chinese were repeating what they had first told the delegation in Peking: "All that's got to go. You Tibetans are even more stupid than we thought. Attaching so much importance to this trumpery!" When I asked him why there were so many pilgrims on Barkhor and in the monasteries, Lobsang reflected for a while and then said: "The Tibetans have slipped through the fingers of the Chinese; the Chinese can no longer control them, especially now that the practice of religion has once more been permitted. We are a very stubborn lot."

Except that the inhabitants of Lhasa, as I noticed during my visit, are evidently still cautious and mistrustful of the peace.

Lobsang Samten, his wife Namlha and their two children no longer live in a comfortable apartment in the United States, but in Dharamsala in a narrow dusty street lined by small and primitive clay houses and wooden shacks. Dogs roll in the dirt, chickens cluck, and hippies carry their babies on their backs like the natives. Here, in this provincial setting, is the home of the Dalai Lama's brother and his wife from the distinguished noble family of Tsarong.

A steep narrow concrete staircase leads to their two modest rooms, one of which doubles as an office. There is no light on the stairs; you have to use a flashlight. When their children began to show more interest in Coca-Cola and ice cream in the States than in Tibet's cultural heritage, the parents decided to turn their backs on the comforts of the United States and to return to where their roots were. These intelligent parents now serve the Dalai Lama at the Dharamsala medical center.

One can well imagine that not all Tibetans abroad will make the decision. I know of a family in Switzerland, whose efforts had earned them middle-class affluence and a spacious house in a residential neighborhood. Then they too thought of returning to Asia; they sold their entire property and decided to build a small hotel in Nepal, close to the Tibetan frontier. The menfolk of the family, who had lived in Switzerland as simple workers, were delighted to be returning shortly to their native surroundings. Piled high with European household equipment, the wife and the children set off for India. The men stayed behind in order to make a little more money; they would follow soon. And what happened? Before a year had passed they were all back: the children, in particular, could not stand it and were clamoring to get back "home" to Switzerland.

An isolated instance, certainly—but one has to face the fact that this is not an exceptional case. Not everyone has the kind of motivation possessed by the more intelligent Tibetans, and more especially the members of the Dalai Lama's family.

The Enigma of
the Reincarnations

I am often asked if there will be Rinpoches in the future. Will another Dalai Lama be born? I always unhesitatingly answer in the affirmative, as reincarnations may occur anywhere—in Bhutan, Nepal, Sikkim or Ladakh, in India, or perhaps even in Western exile. Certainly there will not be the full 1,000 reincarnations revered in the Tibetan religious world, but the major and famous reincarnations will surely continue to occur. Some of them exist already, such as the young Pema Lingpa, whom I met in Sikkim with his teacher and companion, and who lives in a monastery in Bumthang region as one of the highest reincarnations in Bhutan. He is the reincarnation of a fifteenth-century blacksmith who was introduced to religion by divine providence.

I believe that these new reincarnations will have to face more difficult tasks than their earlier incarnations. As they belong to Tibet's natural aristocracy they have first of all duties, and only then do they have rights. Their task is to concern themselves with man's ethical purpose. That means not living for their faith in isolation but keeping alive the Buddhist religion, for in Tibet religion has always been indissolubly linked with politics.

In the Tibetan schools of the "Red Hats" most of the monks have always married, lived in the monasteries with their families and tilled their own fields. The members of the Yellow School, who, like the Dalai Lama and two of his brothers, are high reincarnations, all observed celibacy. As a result of exile and new living conditions abroad many of them have changed their lives, married and started families. The Dalai Lama's brothers also requested to be released from their vows, but they did not thereby forfeit their exalted rank as reincarnations.

The Dalai Lama will quite certainly be reborn, though probably not in Tibet, as the right conditions do not prevail there today. Commissions of high and learned lamas would scarcely be able to ride out into the country now to discover an exceptional child. Once, after I had become an intimate friend of the Dalai Lama, I asked him to tell me the story of his discovery. I knew that he had been born on July 6, 1935, near Lake Koku-nor in Amdo province. He could not, of course, remember the circumstances as he had been very young then, so he suggested I ask the commander-in-chief of the army, Dzasa Künsangtse. This man told me that the Thirteenth Dalai Lama had dropped a few hints about his reincarnation while he was still alive. After his death he had been laid out in state in Buddha posture, facing toward the south; the following morning his head was found to have turned toward the east. In the absence of any more precise indications the Regent eventually traveled to Lake Chö Khor Gye, an eight days' journey, because it was said that the future was reflected in the lake's surface. There, in fact, he had a vision of a three-story monastery with golden roofs, with a small farmhouse by its side. Thereupon groups of specially chosen monks, each with a secular official, set out on a search in the direction indicated. They had with them old and well-worn personal belongings of the Thirteenth Dalai Lama as well as the same objects in resplendent and new condition. They found a number of young boys, but none of them met the requirements. After a long journey they at last came across that three-storied monastery with its golden roofs, and next to it, just as in the Regent's vision, stood a small farmhouse. The gentlemen exchanged clothes with their servants in order to get into the farmhouse kitchen unrecognized and without causing attention; that was where children would normally play. Everything worked miraculously. A two-year-old rushed up to the monk who wore the Dalai Lama's prayer rope around his neck and exclaimed: "Sera Lama! Sera Lama!" The astonishing fact that the child was not deceived by the servants' clothes and that he instantly identified the strangers' place of origin, the Sera monastery, seemed an infallible sign to the monks. Nevertheless, they immediately subjected the boy to the prescribed tests, all of which he passed impressively. Certain of their success, they reported their discovery to Lhasa, in secret writing, via China and India. The Tibetans had to pay a huge ransom for the Dalai Lama, principally to Ma Pu-feng, and in the late summer of 1939 the delegations returned to the capital with the boy and his family.

The Dalai Lama has two sisters and four brothers, all of them above average and gifted. Thubten Jigme Norbu, the eldest brother, had been identified as an incarnation long before the Dalai Lama was found. He, too, was addressed as Rinpoche, but after his flight from Tibet he was released from his vows by the Dalai Lama. Jointly with him I wrote the book *Tibet Is My Country*, the history of his family. Meanwhile he has become a translator and professor at Bloomington University in Indiana, and with his wife and three splendid sons leads an exemplary life. His wife is a member of the most ancient Tibetan noble family of Sakya, whose head and his wife share with the Dalai Lama the privilege of being carried in a litter.

Some time ago in Ladakh, I met Sakya Rinpoche in his monastery of Meru Gompa; he attends there only for great ceremonies, while normally living near Dehra-Dun. Unlike other Rinpoches, who are reincarnated, his title is inherited from one generation to the next.

Thubten Jigme also visited his native Amdo after the cultural revolution and was shocked to discover that all that was left of his former monastery of Tagtsher were ruins.

The second-eldest brother, Gyalo Thöndup, was not an incarnation. He was at school in China and did not visit the capital afterward—at least not while I was there. He was greatly interested in politics; he married a Chinese girl and for a while they lived in Formosa.

The third brother, Lobsang Samten, was a simple monk; he is married to Nanlha Tsarong.

Ngari Rinpoche, the youngest brother, is a high incarnation and possesses eight monasteries in Ladakh alone. Questioned about his views on the theory of reincarnation, he answered somewhat guardedly—but there can be no doubt about his being a reincarnation.

Quite recently I received again a printed invitation from a proud and happy parental couple to attend the official confirmation of their son Tenzin Nueden as a Rinpoche.* The family of this three-year-old incarnation lives in Switzerland and provided the answer to the question of whether reincarnations continued to occur to this day. The Dalai Lama's teachers had acknowledged the child as a reincarnation, and, on his European tour in 1982, the Dalai Lama himself was able to give him his agreement and blessing. Everything now follows its centuries-old course: the boy is given a teacher and lives with him in a monastery. During the last years alone in Switzerland some five incarnations have been born. Most of them reside now as Rinpoches in the mountains of Sikkim and Mysore in India.

Having a child who is an incarnation is a hard blow for some parents: I know of one family, also in Switzerland, also with an exceptionally gifted child, who—in spite of the great honor—anxiously hid the boy away so that they need not hand him over. The parents of Drigung Chetsang Rinpoche, Dadul Namgyal Tsarong III and Yangchen Dolkar,* had been similarly torn between honor and faith on the one hand and separation from their child on the other. For the mother especially the parting was terribly hard when the monks took the little boy away with them to the Drigung monastery, 160 kilometers (100 miles) from Lhasa, to be educated there.

In the past, as today, exceptional children have invariably been sought out and discovered, acknowledged as incarnations and appropriately educated. And as long as there are any believing Tibetans, there will always be incarnations.

*See the book *Der Rinpotsche* (Pinguin-Verlag).

TIBET'S
LOST CHILDREN

A young woman in the dress of the Tibetan nobility was standing in the midst of a crowd of cheerful children. In a warm, solemn voice she was singing an ancient song from their homeland. The woman was Pema Gyalpo, the Dalai Lama's younger sister and director of a big educational center in Dharamsala, with its own nursery and crèche. All around the sports field stood a number of neat houses from which children's voices were heard. Each house bore a plaque with the name of its donor; the name most frequently encountered was that of Gmeiner, the founder of the thriving SOS Children's Villages. But we shall let Pema Gyalpo speak for herself:

> The Children's Village was founded by the Dalai Lama in 1960, to benefit those children and orphans whose parents had done roadwork in India or had died on their flight from Tibet. Since then more than five hundred children have passed through the school. The task of our institution is to provide a home for them and to bring them up in our deep-rooted culture, so that they grow up as Tibetans. The majority are orphans or semi-

orphans. Lately we have had a big influx of children whose parents had been permitted to leave Lhasa for India on a pilgrimage. Although the Tibetans had to give the Chinese an undertaking that they would return, many left their children behind in order to have them instructed in Tibetan culture, writing and language—all of which is impossible in Tibet itself. At present we have 277 such children in the Village. Naturally, the Tibetan parents are questioned on their return to Lhasa about what had become of their children, but they invent all kinds of stories. They had died, or had stayed behind with relations in India. These parents take great risks, and it is touching to see them coming to the Dalai Lama to ask him to accept their children into the Village so that they should remain Tibetans.

Lately the Chinese have instructed parents not to take any juveniles with them on pilgrimages to India. That is the reason why, over the past five or six months, we have only had a sporadic intake of teenagers. But we are still getting babies, and also young people over eighteen. It is quite obvious, therefore, that the Chinese do not want youngsters to leave Tibet.

We owe a lot of gratitude to the Indians. They have been exceedingly helpful, and there are now 100,000 of our refugees here. The people have been given plots of land and have been allowed to establish schools. The Indians treat us so well that they do not even insist on the children being returned to Tibet, though the Chinese are demanding it. In the event of the Chinese continuing to press for the return of the children, their parents in Tibet have already sent word to us that they themselves might formally have to request us to return the children, but we should take no notice of such requests and keep them here.

Of course, we are also dependent on the West and we receive financial support from Europe, America and Australia. Without that help we could not exist at all, and we hope that such help will continue to be given. We are grateful for any publicity we can get. However, a new problem has begun to emerge for us: we now have so many grown-up youngsters who have finished secondary school, and some even university, that it is difficult to find jobs for them. We have reached a point where we are desperately trying to find employment for them, and we are thinking about setting up a small-scale industry. Although a lot of Tibetans were given land by India, that acreage has not increased whereas the number of Tibetans has risen enormously. That is why some small-scale industry for the children educated by us and for trained adults would be a useful next step. We might achieve two things in this way: our fellow countrymen would find jobs, and overpopulation in the Tibetan settlements would be relieved. At the moment our school here in Dharamsala is totally overcrowded—but we have a small piece of land in the lower part of the locality, and we are hoping for support to enable us to build further schools there.

One of those children left behind by desperate parents on a trip to India is the boy I spoke to at the Tibetan Institute at Rikon in Switzerland recently—the boy who told me, in an earlier chapter, about his life under Chinese occupation. As his father was employed by the government—he purchased timber in Kongpo province and supplied it to the Chinese—the boy's parents had been granted official permission to travel to India "to visit relations." They used this opportunity for a secret pilgrimage to the Dalai Lama, and left Lobsang Tempa behind. That thirteen-year-old is one of the fortunate children who have relations in Switzerland—it had been their financial help that enabled him to go there. Another stroke of luck for the youngster was the fact that a Swiss took charge of the boy, found him a place at the Rikon monastery, and now has charge of him on weekends, which are spent in rural surroundings with his own children. At Rikon he is taught by Tibetan monks and made familiar with Tibetan culture. His foster father sees to his European education. Thus this talented youngster represents an ideal case of a man who will be able, one day, to return to Tibet with new knowledge and skills.

The first school for Tibetan children was opened in Mussoorie, northern India, in March 1960. That same year a nursery for orphans was set up in Dharamsala, also in northern India, by Tsering Dolma Takla, the Dalai Lama's elder sister. The nursery later grew into the Tibetan Children's Village mentioned above, run since 1964 by Pema Gyalpo, the Dalai Lama's younger sister. Over the years, the Children's Village has developed into an important educational and training center for Tibetan children. Since 1972 it has been a member of the International SOS Children's Villages. At present it houses more than 1,200 Tibetan children and juveniles entrusted—as mentioned above—to the Dalai Lama's care.

In 1963 the Tibetan Homes Foundation was established in Mussoorie. Here homeless refugee children were accommodated in hostels, divided into groups led by Tibetan houseparents. This institution, too, has been a member of India's SOS Children's Villages for a number of years; it has some 700 children in twenty-eight hostels at present (according to Gyaltsen Gyaltag, *Der Weg zum Dach der Welt*).

22

IN SEARCH OF
OLD MEMORIES

The Tibetan New Year had been celebrated shortly before my arrival in Lhasa in 1982. I had, in fact, hoped to attend it, for it was listed on our group travel program. But there were no New Year celebrations for me. On some flimsy pretext our departure from Europe was postponed to a later date: "There are not enough service personnel for tourists at a time of popular celebrations . . ."

There had been talk of great New Year festivities being planned—but eventually they were quite insignificant. Why was the great *thangka* not hung out on the Potala? That used to be the highlight of all the festivities I witnessed in Lhasa, including of course the New Year celebrations, when it would be unfurled on the last day of the second month.

As I knew that the banner was kept in the small yellow house at the foot of the Potala I wanted to know why it was not simply taken out from there. At first sight the explanation seemed plausible: hoisting this gigantic brocade-and-embroidered-silk *thangka* required not only 200 strong men but they also had to be skilled in the task. This skill was possessed only by the monks from Namgyal Dratsang, whose monastery was in the western part of the Potala and who were now part of the Dalai Lama's inner circle at a small monastery in Dharamsala, where they participated with him in the great ceremonies. Ngari Rinpoche described these Chinese excuses as a "ridiculous pretext."

It may be that the New Year will again be celebrated in Lhasa someday—but not in the manner I had witnessed. Once again I realized how much had been irretrievably lost. In the old days everybody crowded in to attend the festivities—merchants and officials, peasants and nomads in their beautiful ancient costumes. This was Tibetan life, genuine and unadulterated. Rich and poor, they all made their way devoutly and with no inner doubts, to offer to the gods and invoke their blessings. The more magnificent the garments, the more precious the jewelry of the women, the greater was the pleasure of the gaping crowd who knew nothing of class struggle or envy.

For weeks the people sang and danced under the benevolent eyes of the monks. In every home there was a banquet, and Aufschnaiter and I would be invited. In the Deyang Shar courtyard of the Potala the black-hatted dancers gyrated to the strains of Tibetan music, and on the uppermost floor, behind a transparent yellow curtain, the Dalai Lama sat enthroned, contentedly watching his people. One floor below him sat the Regent, arrayed in gold brocade; below him, according to rank, were the ministers, the Dalai Lama's relations and the noble families. Opposite them was the place for the representatives—British, Bhutanese, Nepalese and Chinese. All that is now merely a memory.

I saw prayer flags flying on top of Chagpori, but they were flying over ruins and I was unable to discover who had been courageous enough to set them up there. The medical school on the summit of that mountain was destroyed at the time of the 1959 rebellion—not by the Red Guards. Nor did I see the five great *chötens* of Bargogaling at the western entrance to the city, which had been the doorway to a new life for us ragged fugitives many years ago. Nearly every book on Tibet reported that sentries were posted there, guarding the city. We approached with our hearts pounding—but all we saw were a few beggars stretching out their hands for alms. Certainly no monk-soldiers and no sentinels. We mixed with a group of pilgrims and passed through the gate of Lhasa without hindrance.

That western city gate was another monument destroyed even before the cultural revolution in order to make way for a huge highway. It stood between the Potala and Chagpori. Many a time I would stand at the top of one of these two emblems of Lhasa, watching the women in their festive garb, with their triangular head ornaments set with pearls and turquoise, pouring their libations to the gods. Over their shoulders they carried their brightly colored woven *tsampa* and spice pouches, and soon I inhaled the fragrance of incense made from dried azaleas and juniper twigs.

On my return to Lhasa I searched for the Dalai Lama's spring, where an elephant, a gift from the King of Nepal, used to be taken to drink. The spot was fenced in, but a little water flowed out at its lower end and the people were allowed to help themselves to it. Nothing of it was now to be seen: everything was built up with hutments.

Nostalgia flooded over me as I recalled that romantic spot at the entrance to the city—those massive *stupas,* the central three linked by ropes from which hung dozens of little bells which emitted a silvery note in the slightest breeze. In spite of the arid climate the *stupas* had a marvelous patina and were overgrown with moss. The explanation of this unusual feature in the dry Tibetan highlands were the numerous tiny rivulets which ran everywhere in the old days.

There was also a little pond to the west of the city gate, and the *stupas* were reflected in its surface. On the water of the pool, masses of colorful ducks and other migrating birds would scurry about, and I remember that in winter, when their feet froze onto the ice, pious pilgrims would go down to the lake and carefully free them. Love of all living creatures was great, and because of their belief in rebirth in every form they care for every living thing.

Later, after I had been living in Lhasa for some time, two more *stupas* were erected, and I seized the opportunity to take photographs and make sketches, for the first time ever, of the manner in which such tombs were constructed. Now all five of them—the three central ones as well as the two newly built ones—have been destroyed, and the legend that used to be told in Lhasa has become sad reality. According to this legend the Potala and Chagpori were the head and the tail of a dragon, whose body linked the two hills. When the dragon's body was pierced in order to build the city gate there had been great anxiety among the people, for the legend predicted a disaster for Lhasa if the dragon's body were wounded, and, in order to avert that, the dragon's "spinal vertebra" was repaired by means of these great *stupas*, which were to protect the capital against future misfortunes. Now they have all been destroyed, and disaster has certainly befallen the city.

Time and again I would stop on my walks and ask myself: Is this really the city where I spent so many happy years? Experiences and scraps of conversation long buried in my mind began to reemerge, and one day I wondered if old Amchila—the physician I had so often visited in the past—could still be alive. In point of fact I did meet him again at the Tibetans' new hospital, the Mentsikhang. Delighted, he made me a present of a little herbal whose title page displayed the blue poppy, that queen of Himalayan flowers—a queen not only on account of its beauty but also by virtue of its highly regarded curative powers. To me that blue flower had been the fulfillment of a youthful dream: even as a student in Graz I had sought the "blue flower of romance," which—in the words of the wanderer's song—bloomed secretly beyond the mountains. The flower had been the symbol of my youthful yearning for distant lands, and the song had accompanied me on my expeditions throughout my life. Always, subconsciously, I had hoped to find that blue flower one day. And then, forty years later, I found it in Bhutan. It was the blue poppy, *Meconopsis baileyi,* called thus after its discoverer, Lieutenant-Colonel F. M. Bailey, now a friend of mine. And I saw its brilliant cerulean color in the old doctor's herbal, a most painstakingly compiled little book with Chinese and Tibetan lettering.

The past came back to life during our conversation, and the old physician told me that he and his pupils still walked out into the mountains each autumn to collect herbs. Their favorite spot was Itso, a beautiful lake north of Lhasa that used to be my destination too whenever I went walking with my dog. At that time I had come across a splendid cup-shaped flower whose name I did not know. I have since learned that this was *Saussurea obvallata,* found at an altitude of about 4,000 meters (13,000 feet). I encountered it again a few years ago, by Lake Hemkund, where it bears the pretty name "Brahman Lotus." Pilgrims visiting this sacred lake in the "Valley of Flowers" claim that Brahma had dropped it down upon earth at this spot alone. But Brahma must have done so again, for it blooms just as brilliantly by Lake Itso. Unfortunately there was no time to visit the lake; I only got as far as the Kyetsang monastery, near Lhasa, built into a vertical rock face, yet despite its difficult access, unfortunately destroyed like so many others.

In old Amchila's house I at last—at long last—had some of that good rancid butter tea of the Tibetans. I enjoyed this delicacy of bygone happy days and we sat talking all through the afternoon. We replenished our cups and spoke of the old days.

Amchila had been brought medicines by tourists from America and Europe, and he was glad to have me help him identify them and translate their directions into Tibetan. Out of gratitude he made me a present of his own *menkhug*, the old Tibetan doctor's leather sack, in which the small medicine pouches and instruments are kept. These are very rare nowadays, and this was a valuable gift.

In the old days I had often climbed up Chagpori to the medical school and watched the little monks obediently and attentively following their teachers' instructions. It was a privilege to be a student there, and each monastery would send a number of intelligent boys to one of the two schools. Unfortunately the medical schools at that time had closed their doors to all progress. Learning was strictly laid down, a 2,000-year-old system that could not be changed. It is again due to a Tsarong—this time Jigme Tsarong—that Tibetan science has made considerable progress over the past few years, especially in the manufacture of medicines from herbs and minerals—medicines certainly useful also to us. Nowadays the Dalai Lama's medical center in Dharamsala distributes its natural products throughout the world.

23

Fairy Tales
from the Market

East of Lhasa was Doté, Peter Aufschnaiter's scene of activity, where he had built a canal for a new power station. On my way there I saw some peasants behind their yaks, plowing their fields. They were already equipped with metal plows, provided by the Chinese government to a few peasants. This was easier work than with the old wooden ones to which the village blacksmith would fit a small metal cap. I called out a few friendly Tibetan words to them from afar, and they looked up briefly in surprise.

I again saw the typical fields, not bounded by hedges or trees, and the predominant brown hue of the familiar landscape, and I breathed that crystal-clear dry air that lent all things a sharper focus. This landscape had always had a strange fascination and charm for me: you either love it or reject it; there is no in between. I strolled through it, as if through timeless space, across abandoned land that had once been the home of cheerful and happy Tibetans. I talked to the peasants about the food situation; after seeing those mounds of butter in the bazaar it did not now seem too bad to me. "Oh yes," one of them said, "in Lhasa there is butter, meat and flour. But you go out into the countryside—and you won't find any of them. There the people go hungry." He thus confirmed the findings of the Dalai Lama's delegation. He went on: "All that is for the foreigners, to show them how well off we are." There was also dried yak meat and mutton in the market, but, oddly enough, nobody was buying it. The suspicion could not be avoided that this, too, was just a display for the tourists.

The peasant told me that things had been improving a little over the past three years, and that religion was no longer forbidden. "We are again allowed to pray and make pilgrimages on Barkhor, but it is chiefly the nomads who go there and risk praying and prostrating themselves in public. The inhabitants of Lhasa are still afraid. On no account can you trust the Chinese." We talked about the great monasteries, where thousands of monks used to live in the old days. He listed them all for me: Sera, Drepung, Ganden ... how well I know those names. From this peasant's lips, too, I heard the word *dzüma,* masquerading or sham monks. Everything was *dzüma*— false, swindle, eyewash, nothing to do with genuine freedom of religion. "It's nothing but a Chinese ruse," he complained.

The few monasteries which had not been destroyed were empty. One might chance to see a monk or two, but these would invariably be elderly men; there were no young monks. My peasant kept assuring me how much he and all other Tibetans loved the Dalai Lama, even though they had never seen him. "Religion can now be practiced only on the side—not as in the old days, when it was ever-present."

As for work, even in agriculture, things were less good than in the old days. They had to work collectively and, no matter whether a man worked hard or slacked, they each got the same rations. "In the past, when I worked hard I also owned a lot—isn't that more sensible?" he asked. But certain things had improved during the past three years: above all, they could now grow the crops they really needed.

"At first the Chinese forced us to grow nothing but wheat because their own food consists of wheat flour; hence all the harvest went to the Chinese and no space was provide for growing the barley from which we make our *tsampa*." Now they were allowed to cultivate barley and they again enjoyed working on the land; work once more had a meaning for the Tibetans.

In the bazaar I spoke to a peasant woman, Lobsang Deki. She felt deceived by the Chinese and had no confidence in the present improvement: "Nobody can believe this peace; I had to work in a commune for twenty-three years and only received a small food ration for it. Now I haven't a single square foot of land left, and so I'll leave Tibet and go to India."

I walked on through the bazaar and saw large and small mounds of butter, up to 40 kilograms (88 pounds), which the nomads cut into blocks with a thick wire. It seemed that anybody could buy; one kilogram (2.2 pounds) cost 4 *yüan* (about $2). The traders had carefully placed an old carton over the butter to prevent it from melting under the warm rays of the April sun. Was it all *dzüma*, all show?

On the plain between Shigatse and Gyantse, the most fertile part of the Tibetan plateau, I saw two communes and a few tractors; but whatever tractors I came across, only once was one of them in operation. The others just lay idle. The scenes from the propaganda brochures, of Tibetan girls with makeup and in festive garments sitting on gleaming harvesters, or indeed—in the same elegant getup—operating antiaircraft guns, I never encountered. It seems incredible that a nation such as the Chinese, a nation known throughout the world for its intelligence, for its sages and philosophers, should really consider us such fools as to swallow unquestioningly their Potemkin villages of Tibetan "everyday life."

On the other hand, the extensive irrigation canals, running deep into the side valleys, are exemplary. Diversion of rivers is done in exactly the same way as in the past, by primitive dams. However, countless willows had been planted along the canals, just as Aufschnaiter and I had begun to do on a small scale while working for Chikyab Khenpo, the Chief Abbot. Some of our willows stand to this day; they now have enormously thick trunks. Irrigation is of great value, especially to the Chinese, as it enables them to plant their wheat. But where the Tibetans need water most urgently, in the city of Lhasa for instance, nothing has been done.

Thirty years ago Aufschnaiter and I, on behalf of the government, concerned ourselves with the problem of canalization. We surveyed the whole city, gave each house a number, and drew an exact plan. It will be seen that the Tibetans themselves had this progressive idea long ago; they were just not given the time to implement it.

Three thousand fruit trees have been planted near the barracks, and are being pruned and tended. A Tibetan "gardener" lives in a little house near the plantation; his job consists of chasing off the thieves who, when the fruit ripens, steal it at night in spite of the fence. Here, too, there is no doubt about for whom the fruit is ripening—Chinese or Tibetans. The Chinese, of course.

Everywhere one could see carts being pulled along on bicycle wheels, and occasional bigger ones on old car tires. But one also encountered wagons to which asses or small Tibetan ponies were hitched, up to five animals to one vehicle. In addition to the loads, there were also people crouching on top of them, and it was astonishing that those thin animals did not collapse. Machines, likewise drawn by small horses, were raking the loose gravel back into the cart ruts on the dusty roads—a primitive but useful form of maintenance. The Tibetans working in the fields were just as dust-encrusted and sunburned as I remembered them from the past. And they still carried their baskets on their backs, collecting yak dung and adroitly tossing it over their shoulders into their baskets.

The telephone network had also been improved. The Chinese thought up the idea of building towers of clay bricks and running the wire along their tops. In the old days wooden poles had been used, and these had often been stolen for firewood; the wire would be disconnected and used for securing caravan loads to the beasts of burden.

The nomads, conspicuous in the bazaar by their heavy sheepskin coats which they wear over naked bodies, have lived on the Tibetan plateau since time immemorial, moving from one grazing ground to another to keep their beloved animals healthy and well-fed. The occupying Chinese called them "uncouth hordes" and prohibited their migration, even to neighboring grazing. There has been an improvement in this respect too: they are again encountered with their sheep on mountain passes but some of them are now wearing the green caps of the Chinese.

Even so, they are not entirely free. They are organized in communes, receive an allocation of barley flour and instructions on how many sheep they may slaughter for their own consumption. How different from the old days, when they ranged over huge distances as free men. They would be found sitting cross-legged on soft antelope skins in their small tents woven from black yak hair, contentedly drinking their rancid butter tea, and telling each other the stories which had traveled to them all the way from the south of Tibet, from the Himalayan regions. Tales of the yeti, whom they called *migö* and whom they believed to be a gigantic snowman; fables spread throughout the world ever since exploration began. The Tibetans used to tell many legends about the *migö*, whose "human footsteps" they had discovered—only far, far bigger than those of a human— a creature supposedly sitting down at a fire in the evening, in total silence, eating with the humans, and leaving again, upright as we.

I too have seen such "abominable snowman tracks" in the Himalayas, but it is obvious to me that the yeti does not exist and that the footsteps have a quite different explanation. They are bears, of which there are at least three species in the Himalayas. There is the man-eating bear, the *Shatom,* which will attack humans, and the plant-eating *Tsatom.* Both rise and stand erect on their hind legs, like huge humans with their arms raised. I had encounters with bears myself, and they left mysterious-looking tracks in the snow. This too can be explained. The enormous size of the tracks is due, for one thing, to the snow melting along the edges and, for another, to the fact that the heavy bears place their rear paws immediately against the back of their front paws. Thus the impression arises that these are the tracks of a creature walking on two legs. To make matters even more mysterious, some stories allege that the tracks of the yeti will suddenly come to an end in the middle of a snowfield—but there is an explanation for this too. These are not the tracks of bears but the imprints of the feet of the gigantic *lammergeier,* also known as the bearded vulture, which takes off from the ground after a hopping run.

On the Tibetan high plateau there is another large bear, which digs for mouse hares. I have frequently seen this bear in the distance, digging around in the ground for the little hares and consuming its prey. If disturbed, it would rear up to a man's height. These are unromantic explanations of mysteries which, like the Loch Ness Monster, continue to engage human fantasy.

One of the aspects of progress in Tibet is the fact that the nomads also are able to use the new roads—which is why they are seen again on pilgrimages to Lhasa. It is a scene from the old days—those proud muscular men with their bold manner, and those cheerful apple-cheeked women bartering away in the bazaar. The nomads are once more allowed to roam: this is their way of life and that is what they need for their happiness. The Chinese have evidently come to realize that it would be a mistake to impose any other lifestyle on them, just as I consider it a great mistake for Europeans traveling the world as tourists and missionaries to believe that our morals, religion and way of life alone are right, and therefore worth propagating. During my stay in Tibet I never experienced anything of that sort from the Tibetans. They are a homogeneous religious community, filled with self-assurance, but they have never tried to export their religion the way we do—neither their religion nor their customs and traditions. In all those years, I cannot recall a single instance of any Tibetan wanting to convert Aufschnaiter or me to Buddhism.

RETURN TO
GYANGTSE

We were driving to Shigatse via Gyangtse. Under a blinding sun, in a brilliant pure light, the full glory of the Tibetan plateau was spread out before us. This landscape seems to be tailor-made for the Tibetan religion. Or is it that the Tibetan form of Buddhism could only have arisen in this landscape? It is amazing how peaceful this scenery seems to the viewer, even though it contains all the elements of wildness. We saw only a single tractor on our trip; yaks are still being used in the fields.

The market of Gyangtse, once a famous trading post, has lost much of its former liveliness. Gyangtse used to be the place where the best carpets and textiles were made; a factory is again operating at the foot of the ancient fortress, but this now belongs to the commune, and the classical flower motifs on the carpets have been replaced by dragons and other Chinese symbols.

I well remember the cheerful songs of the women carpet makers, not unlike the humorous *Gstanzl* verses extemporized in Austria. One such song, freely rendered, said something like: "The fidelity of the Gyangtse girls is not as durable as the cloth they weave . . ."

The songs of the Tibetans today are politically colored, like this one:

Tibetans now are like young chicks
abandoned by the mother hen
in a wasteland.

> *Oh may the savior, Tenzin Gyatso,*
> *soon return to Tibet!*
> *Prayers by day! Prayer by night!*

The savage cry of the "black pigs"
is getting fainter. Seize the opportunity!
Prayers by day! Prayers by night!
Prayers throughout the past twenty-three years:
early return of Tenzin Gyatso
to the snow-adorned country.

> *May the religious centers flourish*
> *in the land of religion and may Tenzin Gyatso*
> *live a thousand years!*

Tenzin Gyatso is the name of the Dalai Lama; "the savage cry of the 'black pigs' is getting fainter" is a reference to a relaxation of Chinese oppression.

Unmarried Lhasa girls sing about choosing a bridegroom:

Choose, if you can, a Seei-Chei;
no matter if his face
is pockmarked.

But if you can't, then
Drah Sheei *workers*
are not the worst.

Not worth having are
"irresponsible collaborators":
yet grains of gold
are sometimes found in sand.

"Seei-Chei" is the Chinese term for a driver. A driver earns slightly more than other Tibetans in lowly positions; besides, getting about a lot, he is in a position to come by foodstuffs in excess of his ration. The *"Drah Sheei"* are workers who, though very poor, are well able to bear the rigors of working conditions under the Chinese but would never make friends with them. The "irresponsible collaborators" are the "two-headed ones" mentioned earlier: they should normally be ruled out when a girl chooses a bridegroom—however, "grains of gold are sometimes found in sand," i.e., a suitable partner might even be found in that category.

To return to Gyangtse. The monastery has been razed to the ground, except for two temples and the great *stupa*, which survive. It is said that Tibetans, too, were made to participate in this devastation. It is difficult for an outsider, one who is not involved, to form a judgment. I would prefer simply to report the fact.

During my recent stay in Tibet I saw only one picture of Mao, and that was in the big carpet factory there in Gyangtse. The factory itself is equipped just as it was in the past. A few youngsters would be wearing small Mao badges—but this means nothing, and they would just as readily wear any other buttons. In fact I remember that, in the old days, even officers of the Tibetan army, which did not go in for decorations, would get hold of some badges just to have a splash of color on their chests.

We viewed the surviving parts of the monastery. In the meantime our Chinese guide went off with a gun to shoot pigeons, and a rather touching thing happened: a few Tibetan children ran over to him and tried to stop him from doing so. Surprisingly the Chinese complied and, with some embarrassment, hid his gun under his tunic. During our sightseeing tour they were just emptying the privies—raised platforms with slits within a wall. All the waste, including ash, is thrown down there; the result is good manure for the fields—the only manure, in fact, since the precious yak and cow dung continues to be laid out on walls and rocks for drying and subsequent use as fuel. The country has not become any more hygienic under the Chinese, and there are just as many stray dogs as there were in my days, even though the Chinese are claiming the contrary. In the Kyichu, for example, the river that runs past Lhasa, I saw the swollen corpses of cows lying in the water at two places. That would never have happened in the past, because the river then was the source of our best drinking water.

Again we had to pay if we wanted to take photographs. Here, in the surviving temple of Gyangtse, they even wanted 10 *yüan* per snapshot. I had my 1950 drawings with me in my luggage, so I was able to make a melancholy comparison. However, the two ancient leather-wrapped *thangkas* were still there, and I spent some time in the well-preserved library studying and taking photographs of the magnificently carved and gilded bookcovers. The *stupa* alongside the great temple is one of the biggest in Tibet and is still intact. It is of granite, with five stories. At the different levels are numerous chapels decorated with statues, and a spiral staircase inside leads all the way up into the roof.

On this occasion I was never alone even for a minute: invariably an attendant hovered beside me to make sure I observed all the prohibitions proclaimed on the boards. Inside the temple, two monks were engaged in organizing the endless queues of pilgrims anxious to go to the altar. I was quite sure these were men disguised as monks, not real ones. Of course, I wondered where all the money was going that the tourists had to pay out everywhere. The Chinese assert that it all goes to the Tibetans—yet in the Potala I was given a receipt that was made out in Chinese characters only, so I assume that it is not the Tibetans or the monasteries that receive the tourist money but the Chinese.

When I had to leave Lhasa in mid-November 1950, I also came to Gyangtse with my caravan. One of my best friends, Wangchuk Surkhang, was one of two *dzongpöns* of the city, and he invited me to stay with him as his guest. The fortress, which had been destroyed by the British as early as 1904, was later repaired. Nowadays one room with various exhibits recalls the Young-husband "expedition." Opposite the Dzong rock is the monastery town, composed of eighteen temples. Once a year the great festive *thangkas* used to be hung out there. Nowadays only two of the eighteen temples survive; the others have been destroyed.

As we approached the temple entrance I was pleased to observe that Tibetans were busy restoring the figures of a lion and a tiger. Delighted, I called over one of my fellow travelers; I was genuinely convinced that I was witnessing evidence of the "thaw," the men were so busy smoothing the clay on the now finished lion. A little later I drifted away from the group to have another look at that lion: imagine my surprise when I discovered that all the artists had vanished. I began to nurture that suspicion which Lobsang Samten was subsequently to confirm when I talked to him in Dharamsala. He told me that he had seen the same restoration job in progress two years previously. The moment they caught sight of me the artists came running back and once more got down to "restoring."

That earlier time in Gyangtse, in the late autumn of 1950, I found out, from runners carrying the news to my friend the governor, about the great festivities with which the whole of Tibet was celebrating the young Dalai Lama's assumption of the government. Until that date, all power had been with the Regent. The ceremonies began in Lhasa on November 17, but, in view of the gravity of the situation—the Chinese had already marched into eastern Tibet—were to go on for three days only. Even so, it was a joyous occasion: never before had so much hope been placed in a Dalai Lama's assumption of power. The young ruler was above all cliques and intrigues, and had already furnished proof of his clear-sightedness and resolution. His inborn instinct would make him choose the right advisers and prove him resistant to any attempts at manipulation by self-seeking individuals. Sadly, I was aware that it was too late. He was assuming office at a moment when destiny had already decided against him.

Wangchuk Surkhang, my generous host, was the son of the first marriage of the lay Foreign Minister, Surkhang, with a noblewoman. He had two older brothers of whom one was a cabinet minister and the other a general. The old gentleman, Surkhang, was well disposed toward me and I used to visit his house frequently. Wangchuk Surkhang was also a close friend of Wangdü, which was another reason for our friendship. We did a lot of things together; although he was a little on the plump side, we used to climb mountains and to swim in the rivers together. Unfortunately he smoked opium, and I always tried to make him give it up. But he suffered from stomach pains and claimed that opium was the only effective medicine. Later, he too fled from the Chinese; in Kalimpong he married a Bhutanese girl who bore him a son. Soon afterward he died. His son was recognized as a reincarnation, and lives in the Rumtek monastery in Sikkim.

These close ties with Gyangtse made it almost unbelievable to me that I should now be visiting it in the role of tourist, gaping at what used to be my life. I remembered an incident from the old times: on my last stay there—I was already fleeing from the Chinese—a monk had quietly crept into my room at night and told me that he had over 100 ancient bronzes for sale which had belonged to the Panchen Lama. They were packed in two leather-padded crates which a servant had brought back to Tibet from China. I have no idea what became of them; most probably they are lost.

At a later date, after I had left Tibet, Gyangtse experienced a violent natural disaster. One night the monsoon rains suddenly caused such an inundation that hundreds of people, including some members of the Indian trade delegation, perished. Under pressure of the rains, a natural dam in a tributary of the Nyang Chu burst open, and the water descended like a tidal wave. One of the most delightful women, Kela Pünkang—a participant in every dance that was held in Lhasa, and sister-in-law of Princess Kukula of Sikkim, also lost her life in the floods. Another victim was my friend Rimshi Pemba, who held the fourth rank of Tibetan nobility and was employed by the Indian mission. Every two or three years he would ride to India on leave. On one occasion, when he returned from such a trip, he brought a new Leica to my house with the urgent request: "You know so many nobles; please help me sell the camera. It has brought me nothing but domestic trouble. My wife has been accusing me of throwing my money down the drain instead of saving for our many children. To restore domestic peace I've got to sell this camera!" I was thrilled at the thought of becoming the owner of such a valuable camera but I did not have enough money. So I went to Wangdü and proposed to him that the two of us together might buy it and use it jointly. Subsequently I bought Wangdü out and the camera became my sole property. It enabled me to take those pictures of ancient Tibet which are now of such incalculable documentary value. Wangdü had used the Leica, surreptitiously, to take photographs of a ceremony but he was caught in the act, accused of behaving like a foreigner and demoted.

I found it difficult to tear myself away from this spot charged with so many memories, and I hesitated over whether to leave or not. The decision was made for me by our tour guide, who called for our departure for Shigatse.

SHIGATSE—
OR WHAT REMAINS OF IT

On the road from Lhasa to Shigatse via Gyangtse we passed Yamdrok Yumtso, a strangely shaped lake, on whose banks stand the ruins of the Samding monastery, once the residence of Tibet's only female reincarnation, Dorje Pagmo. In the hierarchy of incarnations she holds approximately the fourth place; in other words, she is a very high reincarnation. In *Seven Years in Tibet* I mentioned that I had frequently seen her on Barkhor or at ceremonies. She was then an inconspicuous young girl of about fifteen, who always wore particularly beautiful clothes and who was in Lhasa preparing for her life as a nun. As a reincarnation she was the holiest woman in Tibet, and wherever she appeared people would ask her to bless them. Her earlier incarnation had performed a miracle in 1716, when Dzungar Mongols threatened her monastery. She had turned herself into a sow, the monks into boars, and the monastery into a pigsty. The Moslems with their distaste of anything to do with pigs gave the sacred building a wide berth. Ever since she has been reincarnated as a young girl.

I had always translated the name Dorje Pagmo as "Thunderbolt

Sow," a term I have used thus in Tibetological literature. *Dorje* is a thunderbolt or a diamond scepter, and *pagmo* is the female of the pig. Quite recently, however, during a conversation in a monastery, a young Tibetan took me up on this point and with a Tibetan-German dictionary proved to me that *pagmo* may also mean a high female incarnation. The dictionary stated: *Pagmo* or *Pagma* is equivalent to "the One who has ascended," a title of venerable female persons or saints. *Pag* on its own is interpreted as "exalted, excellent, distinguished." Only a Tibetologist would be able accurately to interpret the meaning according to how the word *pag* was written. I myself believe that the commonly used translation is correct.

Dorje Pagmo went to India with the first wave of refugees in 1959 but returned very soon after and allied herself to the Chinese. It is said that by means of her spiritual powers she prevented the drying up of Yamdrok Yumtso. She lived in Lhasa, in disregard of her religious vows married the son of Dong-dö-pa, the brother of Ka-Shö-pa, whom I knew well from the Foreign Ministry, obtained a divorce, had a baby, and permitted herself a rather indulgent life. As she was not particularly pretty she must have had some secret powers, as an incarnation, to attract as many men as she was credited with. Nowadays she draws a salary from the state.

Also situated between Gyangtse and Shigatse is Shalugompa, a temple complex from the thirteenth and fourteenth centuries. Fortunately it has not been entirely destroyed, and it is assumed that what prevented the invaders from wreaking havoc was an inscription, in Chinese characters, on the big statue of Buddha: "You may destroy me but I shall return. Those who destroy me will perish." To my regret I observed that the numerous fine ceramics were carelessly left lying about or were used by children as stepping-stones, on which they played without regard for these precious antiques. There used to be magnificent wall paintings of mandalas and tantric picture cycles in the monastery, but those were behind locked doors. I climbed on a little platform and took some flash photographs through a hole in the clay wall. At present there are seven monks living at Shalu, and there is nothing to indicate its mystic past when the *lung gompa*, the so-called "trance-runners," were trained here for their runs of 100 kilometers (sixty miles) or more without food or drink.

On the way over the passes to Yamdrok Yumtso I saw a few Tibetans digging in the fields. I asked our driver to stop because I was interested in what they could be digging up from the soil in winter. Laughing, they showed me a small sweet potato, a highly prized plant. "*Droma,*" they called out, holding it up. Of course, I knew it: there used to be no altar at the New Year without some of these small sweet potatoes piled high on a dish, amidst other offerings. Apparently, they grew chiefly in this neighborhood, where the fields had some groundwater from the nearby lake. The crop represents quite a good revenue for the locals.

These peasants, like everyone else, begged me for a picture of their beloved Yishi Norbu, as they called the Dalai Lama. It was difficult for me to meet their request as I was being watched by the Chinese. But I knew that most of them had a picture already, and when I asked them to show me their pictures of the Dalai Lama, they rummaged in their clothes and produced a pendant or medallion of the Dalai Lama which they wore around their necks. In response to further questions they also pulled rosaries from their pockets, well-worn and greasy from constant use. I also had a remarkable and deeply moving encounter with a Tibetan who was keeping guard outside a Chinese government building and who, with one hand, seemed to be playing with something in his pocket. He told me that he used to be one of the Kusung Magmi, who were stationed at the Norbulingka as the Dalai Lama's bodyguard. Did he still revere the Dalai Lama? I inquired. He thereupon pulled out a picture of him from one pocket and with the other hand, which I had seen moving in his trouser pocket, he produced his rosary—he had been praying.

Shigatse, Tibet's second-largest city, owed its fame to the nearby Tashilhünpo monastery. This was where Sven Hedin's expedition ended in 1907, when his greatly reduced caravan was held up at Shigatse by the Tibetans and thus never reached Lhasa. While I was living in Lhasa, he gave me this good advice in one of his wise letters: "You have reached the city of my dreams . . . make good use of your time, everything is important and worth recording. Make drawings and do not forget even the seemingly most irrelevant matters . . ."

Of course, I followed his advice, but today I realize that I should have persevered a great deal more—everyday things, for example, which then had seemed to me so ordinary that they were hardly important enough to be recorded. Fortunately, I had taken photographs and made sketches of Shigatse and its fortress, and I could imagine that one day these might well be rebuilt on the basis of these records. Nowadays, Shigatse is reached from Lhasa by car in a day. But I enjoy thinking back to the time when I covered the distance on foot or on horseback, taking five or six days on the journey.

Shigatse too was a scene of ruin and devastation, with nothing remaining of one of Tibet's finest fortresses—no prayer flags and no *mani* walls, those walls engraved with prayer formulas. The colorful and onetime lively square below the castle was derelict. Wherever one looked, new tin-roofed houses were closely packed together. Here, in the past, sat the peasant women with their head ornaments arranged in a big hoop, consisting, according to their means, of precious pearls, turquoise and coral. These arched head ornaments distinguished them from the Lhasa women, whose ornaments were arranged as triangles on their heads.

And now? A few peasant women were still sitting on the ground, offering their wares, but there were no ornaments on their heads. For protection against the sun they had put on old straw hats and caps, and they were offering old amulet boxes at bargain prices. They needed the money desperately and one would have liked to help them, but it was forbidden to export anything of this nature. Even so, some tourists would slip these small items into their luggage. There was also meat for sale, and a few ponies were kicking their heels in the dust before a purchaser led them away on a yak-hair rope. The biggest attraction in the bazaar, however, was a dentist who treated his patients with an ancient treadle drill, surrounded by curious onlookers. The patients did not suffer from bad teeth but merely from vanity. I watched the "dental surgeon" file a groove into a tooth and fit some facings of gleaming metal into it. These facings—cheap but glittering like gold—were laid out on a little table for customers to choose, and next to them lay a hammer and a pair of pliers. A cyclist, who had hoped to wriggle through the crowd, was sent flying through the air and landed in the dirt; the audience split their sides with gleeful laughter. I was glad to see that in spite of all those terrible years the Tibetans had lost none of their happy sense of humor. Good-humored cheerfulness is one of their most striking characteristics. They never miss an opportunity for laughter. If anyone trips up they can be amused for hours afterward. Their schadenfreude is universal, but no malice is ever intended. Their mocking laughter does not stop at anyone or anything.

After my disappointing visit to the bazaar, I walked up to the Tashilhünpo monastery. On my way I missed the long prayer wall with its numerous *mani* stones which had led all the way from the town to the monastery. The monastery itself seemed undamaged and well-preserved; however, to anyone who had known it well it was clear that there had been some destruction there too. A few groups of buildings were missing, but the ground had since been so neatly and skillfully leveled that the unsuspecting tourist would notice nothing. The Chinese leaders seem to have a special gift for concealing ruins from visitors.

Of the six mausoleums of the Panchen Lamas, who used to reside at Tashilhünpo, I could see only one. For generations the Chinese have been playing off the Panchen Lama against the Dalai Lama. The present incumbent, who is two years younger, was brought up in China and was proclaimed by Peking to be Tibet's lawful ruler.

Even though the overall impression of the monastery complex was one of a good state of preservation, a number of essential features were lacking: there was not a single prayer flag flying from the roofs under the blue sky, and even the gigantic flagstaffs with their faded flags were no longer standing in the assembly squares. The very entrance to the monastery has been spoiled by a house with an unsightly water tank on its roof, topped by a big red star.

Inside the monastery complex one cannot roam freely but is shepherded around by guides. The gate to the new palace of the Panchen Lama stood wide open but entry was prohibited. A striking fact also was that the way to the temple of the "Buddha of the future," Jampa—a temple towering above all the other buildings— was blocked by a wall. We were therefore not permitted to approach the famous five-stories-high Buddha. I was content, however, to view the monastery from the distance; I knew every one of those galleries extremely well, having photographed them all in detail in 1950 as the guest of the governor of Shigatse. The Buddha was no longer surrounded by a golden-roofed temple; only the front wall survived. As the great figure was carefully wrapped in plastic and tied up with cords, I took this to be proof that nothing had been destroyed here and that this was simply a case of normal decay. The building had been dilapidated and efforts had evidently been made to protect the statue against the weather until the temple was rebuilt. In fact I saw the carpenters marking out the beams with threads rolled in ink.

In a covered passageway, on the other hand, the printing-block carvers did not seem to be genuinely at work; although they were moving their chisels about, I saw on closer inspection that everything had long been completed. Again just a show for the tourists? There were allegedly several hundred monks living at Tashilhünpo but one certainly did not see them; frequently such totals are arrived at by including all family members, just as they are included in calculating the monks' rations.

One Tibetan confided in me his suspicion that the "monks" escorting us went home in the evenings, took off their habits and donned civilian clothes.

It was at Tashilhünpo that I saw the only novice on my visit to Tibet. I would call him the "demonstration and showpiece novice," for we would meet him time and again, neatly dressed in his red clothes, by the side of a tall handsome monk in lambskin-lined trousers. On one occasion he was carrying knobs of butter, next time he was not, and I was getting increasingly curious. Eventually I asked the older monk in Tibetan: "Where are you from?" He replied: "From Amdo." I continued: "Then you must know a lot of my friends, and also Tagtsher Rinpoche's monastery?" He fell silent and made no reply at all. I wondered whether it could really be only the difference in dialect between Lhasa and Amdo that had cut short our conversation. Shortly afterward he walked off with the novice, and I was reminded, by contrast, of Darjeeling in India, where Drugchen Rinpoche, the abbot of the Sanga Chöling monastery, had told me that they scarcely had room or money to accommodate all the young Tibetans who wanted to become monks.

Like a lesser Potala, the fortress of Shigatse used to tower above the city on its hill. It seemed unbelievable that of this architecturally impressive building only the foundation walls now survived. Worse still, Chinese slogans had been painted on the ruins, in characters no Tibetan could read. This fortress, too, had been destroyed by the Red Guards. They were young people, fanatical and politically indoctrinated, yet highly disciplined: according to the Tibetans they never removed any gold, statues of deities, or other objects of value. But they thought up something that was possibly even worse: they incited the Tibetan population—often at gunpoint—to act: and there can be no doubt that not everyone succeeded in resisting these continuous suggestions and threats, and that many therefore took a hand in the looting of the monasteries and fortresses. In several cases, especially in the major monasteries, the presence of regular Chinese troops prevented destruction and pillage because the Red Guards feared armed soldiers.

Altogether the Red Guards were easily influenced and incited—as indeed young people are all the world over. After the end of the Mao era, the fanatical Red Guards were banished to all points of the compass, to rural areas where they could do no harm. Many of them—older and wiser—now live in Sinkiang province, where they have intermingled as harmless citizens with the native population.

In China, too, the period of the cultural revolution with its Red Guards was a frightful time. University life came to a standstill, for everything was to be leveled—there was to be no more differentiation between an educated, properly dressed citizen and the new revolutionaries.

Now that these mistakes have been admitted, the professors who were subjected to such violence at the time are once more respected citizens and again active in their posts. In Isaac Stern's film *From Mao to Mozart,* a professor of a Shanghai musical college describes his sufferings during the cultural revolution, sufferings not unlike those of many Tibetans. The young Red Guards were so deluded that they regarded it as a noble deed to destroy anything from the past. They were taught that religion and aristocracy had to be liquidated in order to make room for Mao's teaching. The young willingly followed the slogans. During that period of the Red Guards, temples and cultural treasures were destroyed in China just as they were in Tibet, though in China many treasures were saved, since it was easy enough to bury them in the soft soil. After the cultural revolution these treasures gradually reemerged, and today one can see many objects of art in Chinese temples again.

Burying objects was scarcely possible in Tibet's stony ground— but there were ways of salvaging them by sending them out of the country, mainly to Nepal. A few items only are being slowly returned to temples and altars; most of them have been lost forever— taken by the long road to Kathmandu, the principal transshipment point, and thence to the great antique markets of the world.

Now the Chinese keep proclaiming: "The cultural revolution was not our fault; that was the Gang of Four, and we have condemned them." But I do not think we can let the Chinese off so lightly. Such horrible incidents cannot be forgotten so quickly or so readily. Our Peking tour guides, who accompanied us to Tibet, likewise never ceased to blame everything on the "wicked Four" and to protest that they themselves were innocent.

Discussion of the past with Tibetans revealed that they were perfectly well aware of who among their fellow countrymen obeyed the Red Guards' incitements to vandalism and who did not. In Shigatse, too, the ringleader had been well known—but the gods themselves punished him. As he reentered the fortress, that time not for loot but to steal some timber, which in Tibet is rare and precious, the huge columns of the fortress collapsed and buried the evildoer.

On the return drive from Shigatse I experienced a small instance of the severity of the Chinese. For a long time our minibus was forced to drive in the dust cloud raised by a truck which, without its driver's cooperation, we had no hope of passing on that single-track road. When finally, after many attempts, we succeeded in overtaking him, our Chinese driver pulled up in front of the truck. I got out with him and gave the truck driver a piece of my mind, in Tibetan. But the Chinese never spoke a word: he simply demanded the man's driver's license and we drove on. The poor Tibetan was totally crushed; he gazed after us in despair and I was now beginning to feel sorry for him. I thought the punishment decidedly too harsh; after all, loss of his license deprived the man of his livelihood. But it was explained to me that the Chinese had passed a law to the effect that all goods vehicles had to give priority to other vehicles, and that infringement of the rule resulted in the loss of one's driver's license.

Our Chinese guide also showed much interest in my own Tibetan past and kept asking me questions. He had the most incredibly naïve and ignorant ideas of the old Tibet. On one occasion he inquired how many of Chiang Kai-shek's officials had been in Lhasa. "One," I told him, "with a secretary, a radio operator and a cook." There was an embarrassed silence. "Why, then the Tibetans must have been even freer than they are now . . ."

IN THE POTALA

Face-to-face with the Potala, towering above the city, I was reminded of some further objects of my search for the past—the tall slender stone obelisk just below the Potala and the two small pavilions in the Chinese style. These had invariably provided picturesque foregrounds for my old photographs of the Potala and Chagpori. My search for these two witnesses to Tibet's past proved in vain. The pavilions had contained the Dzungaren and Gorkha edicts, and engraved on the obelisk, standing six meters (twenty feet) high in front of the Potala, was, among other things, a decree requiring the Chinese to pay Tibet an annual tribute of 50,000 bales of silk. That was in 763, when Tibetan troops had advanced to the gates of the imperial capital and dictated their own peace terms to the Chinese.

I remembered the little stream, with wild iris blooming on its banks, over which I had built a small arched stone bridge. Alongside it ran Peter Aufschnaiter's irrigation canal to his newly established tree nurseries. These had become necessary in order to avoid having the large quantities of wood needed for the New Year celebrations lugged over great distances by servants. Vast amounts of firewood were needed to keep the additional 25,000 monks, who flooded into Lhasa at that time of the year, supplied with tea and soup. The Chief Abbot of the country, to whom all monasteries were subject, rather liked our idea of an irrigated tree plantation and commissioned us to build the canal and plant the trees.

My search for the stone obelisk and the pavilions was, as I said, unsuccessful at first, but when I made inquiries I was informed that they had to give way to the new road and had been reerected elsewhere. I did in fact find the column at a point farther to the east; however, it had been surrounded by a wall so that the lower part of the inscription was no longer visible. In vain did I try to get a key to the door in the wall; I was told it could not be found anywhere. Why had the wall been built? Was it really, as some Chinese claimed, to protect the magnificent obelisk from the many pilgrims who would tap it with small stones in order to take back a few grains of sand, which they believed would bring them good luck, and because that constant tapping had left some slight marks on it? Or was it to stop people being reminded of that long-distant past when China had to pay tribute to the Tibetans?

Eventually I also found the two small pagodas; they were now on the northern side of the Potala. I was therefore unable to take a picture of the two small pavilions, against the now destroyed Chagpori, for the purpose of comparison.

I am always asked how it was possible to take photographs in Lhasa thirty years ago. The answer is a roll of over 100 meters (330 feet) of film which I had discovered in a house in Lhasa, left behind by an expedition. Fortunately for me, the dry climate of the Tibetan plateau had preserved it in good condition. But the principal landmarks of old Tibet can be seen not only in my photographs but also on old *thangkas* and frescoes. One of these was the ancient state printing house—another building that I was unable to trace and which had likewise fallen victim to new roadworks. It used to stand in the Shö quarter, directly below the Potala, and produced the magnificent large sacred printed books.

Soon I found myself at the new pool in front of the Potala, a favorite background for Chinese soldiers' posed snapshots for their families back home. Face-to-face with the Potala, the most magnificent structure on earth, I surrendered, as I had done so often before, to its magic. What was the secret of its attraction? Was it the huge scale of its plan, the splendor of its golden roofs towering into the blue sky, or was it the memories it evoked in me? It was all these together, and also the architectural homogeneity that makes this work of art so unique. I saw the two-story yellow house where the two largest *thangkas* were kept. I was assured that they were still there, carefully rolled up, last displayed on the Potala below the red central block in 1959, shortly before the Fourteenth Dalai Lama fled the country. I had to dispel these memories, for I was with a group of tourists and allowed, for an admission fee of 100 *yüan*, to enter the palace to which I used to be a respectfully admitted guest of the Tibetan nation, climbing the many steps to its sacred ruler. The Dalai Lama's words from that time served as an adage for the rest of my life: "Anyone wishing to come up to me must ascend step by step. No one reaches the top in a single leap." The same applies to life: it must be climbed one step at a time if one wishes to attain the top. A single skipped step may mean the end of a road to a great goal.

I paid my 100 *yüan* and we were assured we could take whatever photographs we wished—of course, only in the rooms they allowed us to enter. Our cars were parked at the western end of the Potala and we had approached the palace from its northern side, along the old horse track. Once upon a time, two automobiles with registration plates "Tibet No. 1" and "Tibet No. 2" had used this track—an amiable whim of the Thirteenth Dalai Lama, who, in the 1920s, had these cars, stripped down into their components, carried to Lhasa from India on the backs of humans and yaks, across the high snow-covered mountain passes.

The interior of the Potala struck me like a museum. We viewed the tombs of past Dalai Lamas, *stupas* several stories high inside the building with several tons of gold used for their protection. Trained to observe the smallest details, I spotted a picture of the present Dalai Lama on one of the altars—the first and only such picture I encountered in a public place in Lhasa. I was most interested in the throne room and in the Dalai Lama's private apartments, for it had been there that Peter Aufschnaiter and I had our first official audience with him and the Regent within a few days of our arrival. That encounter in 1946 had been arranged for us by Pala Drönyer Chemo, the Chief Chamberlain.

Thirty-six years later I was slowly entering those familiar rooms, and everything was just as it had been, almost as if the Dalai Lama had only just walked out and might walk in again at any minute. His cope was draped in such a way that one seemed to perceive his figure inside it; from the wall the great reformer Tsong Kapa was gazing at me from a fresco. I looked at the richly carved little tables and recognized his jade teacup, set on a gold stand and covered with a gold lid. But it was empty, and not, in accordance with Tibetan custom, filled in token of an early happy return. I thought of the Dalai Lama's cup in his Dharamsala exile: neither jade nor gold—a simple enamel mug painted with a landscape with yaks. I had watched him over many years drinking the tea of his native Amdo from it. Unlike the practice in Lhasa, where butter is put in the tea, in Amdo it is taken with milk.

I continued to look around and recognized his *tsampa* bowl, turned from the knot of a tree. There used to be a veritable cult of these bowls; the more figuring there was in the wood, the more valuable the vessel. I have seen Tibetans pay collectors' prices for teacups made of such strikingly figured wood.

In the bedroom along the wall stood the Dalai Lama's plain yellow-painted tubular steel bed; by its side, on a chest, stood his clock and calendar, stopped on the day that was his last in the Potala. That was the night before he moved into the Norbulingka, from where he subsequently made his escape. I read the English calendar leaf: Tuesday/Wednesday 31. The clock stood at the fourth hour. An element of movement was introduced into this roomful of memories by a Tibetan polishing the floor with thick felt slippers, performing slow skaters' movements. Indifferent to his surroundings, he was moving through the rooms, and I realized once again how quickly time could turn things into ordinariness once they ceased to be filled with life.

We stepped into the great eastern courtyard, the Deyang Shar, the scene in the old days of the black-hatted dancers, moving in unison before the admiring and respectful eyes of ambassadors and nobles on the spectators' balconies. Now everything looked desolate and untidy. However, as Wangdü—responsible also for the Potala—had explained to me, the ground was being dug up in a good cause. Whereas in the old days water had to be carried up to the roof of the Potala in heavy wooden tubs, by way of ladders and staircases, water pipes were now being installed. A sensible improvement, I thought, remembering the primitive small washbowl then used by the Dalai Lama.

Leaving the Potala, I felt as though I were stepping out of a tomb. I inhaled the fresh spring air deeply. Once more I looked down: in the distance beyond the ruins of the Chagpori I saw the Kyichu with the dam I had built thirty years ago and, farther to the east, I tried hard to make out all the places where I had lived. I saw the Turquoise Bridge surrounded by tin huts. It was difficult to make out the landmarks: so much had been destroyed, and so much had changed. One bright spot, at least, was the new pool in front of the Potala with the little Chinese pavilion. Yet this pleasant sight did not hold me for long; I wanted to rediscover more of my past and I could not stop myself searching for it.

Then, suddenly, I was seized with an urge to run away. Had I really returned to Lhasa? I kept asking myself that question. My malaise at seeing this city again was growing, and I tried to stifle it by reasoned argument. What more did I want? Surely I had known what to expect. Was everything not just as I had known it from pictures and reports? Everything just as I had expected it, and no cause for dismay. The heart of Lhasa, indeed the heart of Tibet, the Tsuglagkhang, was still, radiant, before me.

The Radiant Heart
of Tibet

The air was fragrant with yak-dung fires and damp earth. A barely visible bluish veil hung over everything, lending the atmosphere a special tranquillity, almost an element of transfiguration. I was walking along Barkhor: some of the shops were open, but most of the merchants had spread out their wares—cheap jewelry, colorful rugs, rancid butter—on the ground before them. Along the walls of the houses on Barkhor, the protective ring around the holy of holies, the Tsuglagkhang, sat old men in a variety of clothing, mostly Chinese, turning between their fingers their rosaries with their 108 wooden beads and muttering softly to themselves. I noticed that every so often a nomad would stop in front of them and get them to bless his own prayer beads. I stopped too, looked at the old men, and realized that they were monks, perhaps even learned lamas, for whom there was no longer any room in the destroyed monasteries, and who had returned, homeless, to this spot, solely to pray and to bless, to receive alms, and to be near the holiest of their holy places.

Once more I saw the pilgrims prostrating themselves, circling the

Tsuglagkhang clockwise, some by the length and some by the breadth of their bodies. In the old days they used to protect themselves against the hard stony ground by gloves made of wood and leather; now they were using pieces of discarded tires tied around their forearms. But for the overhead wires waving in an untidy jumble in the air, I could have surrendered to the illusion that everything was just as it had been. For this was the unmistakable Lhasa of the past.

I had reached the northern side of Barkhor, where the big *stupa* used to stand in the open square. Now everything seemed neglected and dirty. The former courthouse, its windows broken and its ground floor bricked up, provided a resting place for a few nomads; sitting on its front steps, they were eating their *tsampa*. In the basement, formerly the city jail, there were no condemned men now. I walked on to the eastern part of Barkhor, where scaffolding up to ten meters (thirty-three feet) high, adorned with ornaments made of butter, used to be erected on the fifteenth day of the Tibetan first month for the New Year festivities. I scarcely recognized the entrance to the house of the minister Surkhang, where I used to be a constant guest in the old days. A new gate had been made of steel tubing and concrete. The courtyard was neglected and filthy, there were no flowers in the windows, only the well in the middle of the courtyard was in use. Just as in the old days, people were lining up to lower their buckets on a long rope for what, after the Chagpori spring, was the best water in Lhasa.

I recognized the former foreign ministry, down-at-heel like everything else. Between it and the main gate to the Tsuglagkhang was a big closed door. That was where the powerful monk-police were housed during the New Year festivities. During those weeks of nonstop celebrations the lay officials would withdraw and the Shengo monks would take over the city's administration and judiciary.

My walk around the Tsuglagkhang completed, I entered its center, the temple with the jewel-studded image of Jo Rinpoche. Access to the holy of holies is barred by a heavy iron chain curtain, but this is now usually raised to the top left whenever pilgrims are circling the statue.

Before the main temple entrance are large flagstones; these are polished to mirror smoothness and are hollowed out in many places—witness to the piety of the Tibetans who, with brief interruptions, have been falling on their faces at this spot for more than a thousand years. Once more we paid 150 *yüan* (around $75) and were told we could take photographs wherever we wished. Was there some malicious intent in this, some deliberate contempt for the Tibetans' holy of holies? To me the idea of tourists moving about here freely, taking pictures, letting off their flashes, and climbing upon railings to make sure of even better shots, was shocking—and yet it was a fact. There was no respect left for the profoundly devout pilgrims; the temple had become a tourist attraction. The air was thick and stifling, smelling of burned oil and human sweat. A far worse crime had in fact been committed by the Chinese in the 1960s—far worse than the present desecration—when they turned this most sacred of Tibetan temples into a cinema and dormitory for visitors.

Shortly after the cultural revolution only a few tourists had visited the temple, inspecting it by the light of weak electric bulbs. Nowadays everything was brilliantly lit, both for the tourists and the streams of pilgrims, by countless butter lamps, which were emitting a flickering light and a great deal of heat. Offerings were so plentiful that the temple guardians, running about in shirtsleeves, were continually obliged to pour off oil and butter into tin canisters. Each pilgrim brought something: oil, butter, barley flour or a *khata*. There was a ceaseless ebb and flow of people bearing offerings. I deliberately did not follow the path kept free for tourists along the walls but mixed with the pilgrims who, pressed tightly together, were making their way around the holy of holies without any pushing or elbowing.

In no other temple in Tibet does one receive the same impression of piety and devotion as in this one, the Jokhang. It was not the Potala that brought these people to Lhasa, it was not even the thought of the Dalai Lama that made devout pilgrims and nomads travel for months. They all wanted to come to this shrine and to touch with their foreheads at least the platform on which Jo Rinpoche's figure sat. I saw faces radiant with faith and happiness—they had at last reached the goal of their dreams.

After the magnificent Jo Rinpoche, the most important figure was the eleven-headed Chenrezi, whose reincarnation is the Dalai Lama. This statue, too, the guardian deity of Tibet, had to be restored after its destruction. Four of the original eleven heads, however, had been smuggled out of Tibet and are now kept, as their most precious relic, in the temples of the Tibetans in exile in Dharamsala.

I also paid a visit to the guardian goddess of Lhasa, Palden Lhamo, and asked a temple attendant to raise for me the silken curtain in front of her face. He did so willingly, and a slight shiver ran down my spine as she gazed on me out of the rigid pupils of her enormous eyes. In the old days she used to be carried around Barkhor in procession, and in the people's minds she possessed similar faculties to those of the state oracle, whose facial expression at the moment of prophecy was similarly uncanny and awe-inspiring.

I inspected some beautiful larger butter lamps, but I missed the precious gold bowls, weighing several kilograms, which a Tibetan minister, who then allowed me to accompany him, had donated in 1949. Despite the serious damage done to the figure of Jo Rinpoche, he was once more magnificent with his glittering turquoises, corals and pearls; the gold again had a warm and precious glow. I felt sure that very few people would be able to find any change here.

One of the most important studies on the Tsuglagkhang was

written by the former Minister of Finance, Tsipön Shakabpa, in Tibetan. He was one of the four senior officials sent on a world tour by the Lhasa government in 1948 in order to stimulate interest in Tibet. Care had been taken to select especially educated and progressive nobles; the world was to be persuaded that Tibet was not inhabited by savages. The whole trip took a year, and the four were courteously received everywhere; but when Tibet needed help against the Chinese the world held back. I have visited Shakabpa in Kalimpong, his present place of residence, and he has given me his work on the Tsuglagkhang and on the history of Tibet, written in exile. In it he has juxtaposed old and new pictures, leaving it to the viewer to compare and make judgment.

What interested me most in the Tsuglagkhang, however, was not the magnificent Jo Rinpoche. I wanted to find the bell which had been left behind by the Capuchins in the eighteenth century and which bore the inscription *Te Deum laudamus*. It had once been suspended from a wooden beam in a passage leading to the shrine, together with many other bells. Some of these were now hanging along the side of an anteroom, but that of the Capuchins had disappeared. A Tibetan suggested that, together with other historical objects, it was locked up in a room of the Norbulingka. The pilgrims now entering the shrine therefore lack purification, for they believe that passing under a bell liberates a man from the wrong way.

I clearly remembered the door in the Tsuglagkhang through which one reached a well which was a sacred place to the Tibetans, the place where the highest government officials came to make their offerings every year. To Aufschnaiter and myself it was obvious that the source of this was groundwater, since the entire Tsuglagkhang had, according to legend, been built on a filled-in lake. I found the door but, as might have been expected, the key again could not be found. At this point I should like to quote Siegbert Hummel, the outstanding scholar famous throughout the world for countless publications on Tibet. In a letter to me he said:

> I have studied that shrine for many years. To me the Tsuglagkhang is by far the most interesting shrine in the world—by far because it has been alive down to the present day. It is conceived like the fortified sanctuaries of the ancient Middle East. The Temple in Jerusalem was such a sanctuary, the chaotic primordial waters below it being exorcised by the sacred shrine. The Tsuglagkhang also has that well-shaft which belongs to the sphere of the Klu [the serpent deities of water and the underground]. The Etruscans also had that shaft, from which issued the roads *Urbi quadrata* to all the points of the compass.

The temple attendants were more concerned with collecting money than with litanies and prayers, and I again suspected that they were museum attendants rather than monks, wearing civilian clothes under their habits. I was also told that on the day the Panchen Lama returned and took up residence at the Tsuglagkhang these guards had fled in panic. One wonders why. Surely because of their guilty consciences.

Up on the extensive roof of the Tsuglagkhang I inspected the two—frequently reproduced—golden deer with the wheel of life. Letting my gaze roam around I came to the conclusion that not very much remained of the former splendor and glory. From up there I could only surmise the state of the room where the four cabinet ministers used to have their meetings; what I could make out looked weatherworn and suggested newly healed wounds. Some distance away I heard the rhythmical pounding of round stones, fitted to a pole, being struck against the cement-type floor in unison by men and women, who were repairing it in this manner. They were cheerfully singing songs I knew from the old days. Singing and music making were part of their lives, and not even the Chinese could silence them.

The Tsuglagkhang building with all its temples and architectural splendors, the gigantic structure of the Potala—these represent an enormous achievement by the Tibetan people, erected over the centuries, often by serf labor. They might have endured for thousands of years yet had not so much been destroyed by human hand. Who would venture nowadays, be he ever so powerful, to create such buildings? And in spite of the demystification of these places by camera-clicking tourists, everything still has a mystical enchantment. Even the most insensitive person must experience here a kind of revelation, stand amazed, in wonderment, and gain an idea of something he had previously known only in books. I believe that anyone visiting the Tsuglagkhang will experience the fulfillment of a lifelong dream—the lure of Tibet.

THE THREE PILLARS
OF THE STATE

Ganden, "the Joyful," was not on our program, and efforts were being made to keep us occupied so as to prevent us from seeing any more ruins. The visit was not, however, forbidden and a Nepalese businessman offered to drive me there in an hour and a half. But I did not have enough time; there were still some personal items on my program.

I had seen the pictures taken of Ganden by the Dalai Lama's delegation, as well as the photographs of Manfred Abelein and Peter-Hannes Lehmann, in which one can indeed make out a few new wooden beams amidst Ganden's wrecked buildings. I had also heard ceaseless assurances by the Chinese that the monastery was being rebuilt and that 320 monks were already living there, though admittedly there were no novices.

The image of Ganden's destruction cannot be chased away. With the best will in the world, how can reconstruction ever replace what has been ruined? Where could one find such magnificently carved wooden bookcovers, such enchanting statues of deities created with a spirit of deep faith by the most talented artists over hundreds of years; who could possibly re-create those magnificent frescoes painted in natural colors, whose manufacture was an art in itself? Everything in Ganden was deserted now—empty and silent as the grave, wherever one turned. And yet—I am quite sure of this— whatever has survived there, a few frescoes and the dressed-stone foundation walls, still recall riches, faith and power.

It was at Ganden that the old Tibet once more witnessed a moment of glory. There, in February 1959, before the most important dignitaries and scholars, the Dalai Lama submitted to his examinations for the title of professor of metaphysics. For the Dalai Lama that occasion was also a welcome pretext for declining an invitation to the National Assembly of the Chinese People's Republic, which was just then meeting in Peking. Once more the old Tibet displayed its splendor and beauty. If the Dalai Lama were to return one day, things would never be the same on that occasion, when the nobles rode into the monastery town on their caparisoned horses, wearing their gorgeous robes. Never again will there be those red-and-white friezes or those golden roofs, or the brilliant yellow of the awnings against the blue sky. Everything will be different, as indeed it is already.

Drepung, the "Rice Pile," is only partially destroyed, and at the adjoining Nechung, once the seat of the state oracle, I saw quite a number of carpenters at work. Reconstruction was in progress . . . Yet my footsteps echoed eerily from the walls of the empty rooms. I scarcely knew where I was. I was looking for the cells of the Dalai Lama's brothers, who had been at school there. I remembered the many occasions when I had visited Norbu and Lobsang, when I had chatted with them, or eaten sun-dried yak meat and washed it down with the worst butter-tea in Tibet. I had become quite used to that famous beverage, and had come to like it, but here in Drepung they seemed to use the most rancid butter and the worst tea-bricks.

What had become of the beautifully carved wooden tables, or of the silver jugs and teacups chased with good-luck ornaments? What had become of the heavy brocade-framed *thangkas,* what of the abbots and ministers who had such an air of power and severity in their magnificent garments? I was keeping my eyes open for the three novices who were allegedly to be found there, the first since the occupation. But all I saw were small clusters of tourists, sightseeing like myself. Men and women from all over the world, all talking excitedly and at the same time: "Frightful, this destruction, how beautiful those stones are . . ." Not even a shadow of doubt or misgiving crossing their faces. Had they no idea of what had stood here in the past? The day of the great monastery festival, when several of the giant *thangkas* were unrolled! Drepung did not have a special *thangka* wall like, for instance, Tashilhünpo or the lower white frontage of the Potala. At Drepung the *thangkas* were laid out on the ground: to the west of the monastery there was a marvelous slope that was ideal as a place to display the heavy *appliqué* roll of pictures. Numerous monks, and also a few lamas, would carry the heavy roll on their shoulders, and the pilgrims, who had come in vast numbers, would walk past them, as if accidentally touching the sacred object with their hands and foreheads, or symbolically helping to carry it, and thereby acquiring benediction. All over the hillside scattered groups would sit picnicking—noble aristocrats with their red-hatted servants in ceremonial dress, as well as monks and nomads eating their *tsampa* out of little leather pouches. On several occasions I had taken part in these festivities, and I shall never forget the delicious *momos* prepared by Norbu's and Lobsang's servants: finely chopped meat and fragrant spices wrapped in wafer-thin pastry.

Those had always been enjoyable days full of mirth and laughter. Whenever the Dalai Lama came visiting, the incarnations would sit in the front row throughout the ceremonies—a small assembly of living saints. It was in Drepung that I first witnessed those famous logical debates between the ruler of Tibet and the leading scholars. These were part of the most intimate aspects of Tibetan life, and I owed it entirely to my friendship with Lobsang Samten that I was allowed to sit in on these debates by 3,000 monks, to whose faculty Lobsang Samten belonged. Together with the other monasteries there were then some 10,000 monks in Drepung.

There was another feature that drew me to Drepung more strongly than to other monasteries—the athletic contests between the *dob-dobs* of Drepung and Sera. The *dob-dobs* were a small group of athletic monks who smeared their faces with soot to give them a terrifying aspect. Before the contest they would fling off their habits to reveal a short loincloth studded with small bells. As a former sports instructor I was of course tempted to participate in the contests, and the monks gladly agreed. But the men of Drepung were so good that I had great difficulty in keeping up with them in their three disciplines of running, stone-throwing and a kind of long jump. All that was long ago . . .

Now everything looked abandoned and desolate. I was unable to find the 350 monks who were said to be living at Drepung again. No hot steam issuing from the kitchens, where the monk-cooks, their faces soot-stained, used to stir their huge pots over clay stoves fired with brushwood and dried yak dung. No intoning of litanies, no muffled drums. Just a few monks making sure everyone paid his *yüans* for each snapshot.

I bent over every little detail to inspect it at close quarters, whether it was a faded fragment of a fresco or the remains of a baluster, a wood carving, or the paler areas on the wall, where precious *thangkas* had hung or from where gilded statues of deities had looked down on the believers. I picked up a small piece of paint; who could tell how many centuries this fragment in my hands had hung above the heads of the Drepung monks, this tiny piece of "gold" that must have formed part of a statue.

Sera, the "Rose Fence," another of the monasteries forming the three pillars of the state, looked like the well-preserved frontage of a fine city when viewed from the distance. On a closer look, however, one could see the ruins behind it. The monastery had only been partially destroyed; the debris had been tidily removed, but there had been no reconstruction. Of all the treasures shown to us only the statue of Tamdring, the greatest guardian deity of the monastery, was the original; all the rest were later copies.

There were a few tourists scurrying about with their cameras, also a few attendants, but again I sought in vain for monks practicing their religion. True enough, I was told that many of the monks who had fled to their native villages during the cultural revolution, to escape from the Red Guards, were now "coming out of their holes like mice when the cat has retreated a little." As they came mostly from peasant or nomad families they had been able to hide out with their parents and earn their keep by working. Three hundred of them are reputed to be back at Sera, but these figures invariably include family members to ensure appropriately increased food rations.

In Dharamsala, I had a conversation with a monk from the Sera monastery, who told me: "At most there are fifty monks there now. They are married and are said to be permitted to practice our religion, but they are afraid to do so. Most of the monks living there are merely masquerading as monks, while working for the Chinese. As they are not genuine monks they do not read any books, neither do they pray." These were the words of Lobsang Namgye, who fled Tibet as recently as 1981. Time and again he too used the word *dzüma*—everything is sham, only a façade and deception. Nothing to do with religious freedom.

In Sera I saw frescoes which had been destroyed and which were being restored very badly. I also saw others, well preserved, behind wire-netting frames.

Peking is trying to make some reparation. Money has been made available for restoration. A drop in the ocean, perhaps—but evidence of goodwill.

I remember Sera so well because something like a minor civil war broke out between Sera and Lhasa in 1947. There were fears then that the rebellious monks might march into the capital and loot it. Aufschnaiter and I were busy fortifying the Tsarong house, where an ancient machine gun had been mounted against the notorious monk-police from Sera, the *dob-dobs*. My advice was that the whole area around it should be illuminated as much as possible, as brightness would hamper the enemy. The conflict lasted only a few days, and I was soon able to take my Apso dog to Sera again for a peaceful stroll.

On the road to Sera had stood an isolated building, Trabchi Lekhung, where Tibet's postage stamps had been printed and coins struck. Now that house, once alone in a wide plain, was swallowed up in a sea of tin roofs. Nothing attracted me to it now—I knew that during the cultural revolution it had served as one of the most atrocious prisons. East of Sera there was also the place where dead bodies were dismembered; I did not go there now, any more than I had done in the past. Perhaps it was respect for death that had kept me away then as it did now. The Tibetans used to carry their dead there on their own backs; the only aspect of the ceremony that has changed is that they now carry them there by tractor.

Nothing remains of Sera's former splendor and beauty. Only slowly and hesitantly do the first signs of improvement appear. Just as the old monks, at least, are returning to their monasteries, so also prayer flags are reappearing on a few buildings, passes and bridges. Admittedly, in the communes I still saw the occasional flag with the five stars, the Chinese national flag, or a red banner on the roof of a house inhabited by a sympathizer or collaborator. Sometimes one could even find the five-colored prayer flags and the red stars flying side by side in the wind. On the high-altitude mountain passes, where one might feel safely out of sight of the Chinese, religious banners were once more flying in the thousands. They were waving in the wind, alongside the Chinese slogans which had been painted on the rock faces in place of the believers' *Om mani padme hum*.

All these changes for the better are proceeding very slowly and tentatively. As I have said before, people do not trust the Chinese and hardly dare to believe that what had for so many years been punished by death or imprisonment suddenly can be permitted again. Cautiously, however, the Tibetans are digging up their small bronze Buddhas and erecting little domestic altars. Prayer wheels are once more being turned, and colorful prayer flags fly sporadically from roofs and passes. Mao's pictures are being replaced by photographs of the Dalai Lama, brought into the country by his delegation or by tourists, or kept hidden from the Chinese throughout all that time. Now and again I even saw women sowing seeds in the fields, wearing their fine colorful ornaments—until recently frowned upon— though perhaps still a little timidly, remembering the recent past. Not so the Khampas: they were wearing their ornaments boldly and freely, regardless of what the Chinese might say. They had always been an exception, being braver than the inhabitants of Lhasa, who had a great respect for them. They are real daredevils, and their knives come out at the slightest provocation.

An intelligent Tibetan I met in Lhasa kept using the word *temdreme* whenever he referred to Tibet. I would translate it as a "bad state of affairs." He was very pessimistic and thought matters were going badly, *temdre-me,* for Tibet. It was bad to forget old customs and traditions, for Tibetans no longer to wear their fine old garments, or to be afraid to profess their religion. The gods should not be denied, for they would punish the people and send misfortune upon them. He feared, almost prophetically, that the day would come when all their cultural heritage would be lost; there would then be regrets, but like most regrets they would come too late.

The highest Tibetan officials working for the Chinese are Püntsog Wangyal and Ngabö Sawang Chenpo. Püntsog Wangyal comes from Bathang, the eastern and oldest part of Tibet that was first annexed by the Chinese but nevertheless is ethnically purely Tibetan. A patriotic Tibetan, he too spent some time in Chinese prisons. Püntsog has some responsibility for the reconstruction of destroyed monasteries, but he has no power of decision; he can only advise: "Samye or Ganden should now be rebuilt." He enjoys greater popularity and respect, both with Tibetans and the Chinese, than Ngabö, who, even in the old Tibet, had been a haughty and snobbish "noble."

Püntsog is a courageous patriot who stands up for his views—something the Chinese respect and appreciate. Ngabö Sawang Chenpo, though also a patriot, is a very different person, who instantly submitted to the Chinese and whom they, too, regard as a man without courage. Ngabö was the first to collaborate with the Chinese, and it was he who surrendered the Tibetan troops in Kham province to the Chinese.

Püntsog, by contrast, is a cheerful and amiable man who cares about people and talks to them. Both of them, I was told, travel just as much and without hindrance as in the past. They have their servants, their bodyguard, and a cook—in fact, a whole caravan of retainers. The only difference is in their form of transport. Instead of riding across the plains and over the passes on horseback they now travel from Lhasa to Peking by air. Within Tibet they use a four-wheel-drive vehicle.

If life were ever to return to the monasteries, feeding and keeping the monks would become a major problem. At present, in their small numbers, they live on the alms given by the many pilgrims who visit the monasteries again. In the old days these monasteries had been rich and powerful, owning extensive tracts of land which were worked by the people who, while feeding themselves, had to deliver up large quantities to the monasteries. These have now been expropriated, and pilgrims' donations could not possibly be sufficient to maintain an appreciable number of monks; certainly, no help can be expected from the Chinese government. Even the old argument that the monasteries took the place of schools and should therefore be supported by the government is no longer valid in Tibet.

The Tibetans have a proverb: *"Nang-la dra ma-shüna, chi-ki tönta droki mare."* Roughly translated this means: "If there is no unity within, nothing can be achieved outside . . ."

29

TRAGEDY AND
LOYALTY OF
THE PANCHEN LAMA

It is nineteen years since the Panchen Lama was last in Tibet, and no one has been the subject of a greater number of rumors. There has been talk of captivity in Peking, of marriage, or even forced marriage, and his name has again been used for intrigues against the Dalai Lama. What had fed these rumors was the fact that the Panchen Lama had made broadcasts in accordance with the Peking line and that he had repeatedly proclaimed his sympathies for Red China.

The questionable character of such Chinese statements was revealed at the time of the Panchen Lama's return in the spring of 1982, when he once more regarded himself wholly as a Tibetan and when he was enthusiastically welcomed by the people. The Dalai Lama himself, in all his conversations with me, had invariably expressed his sympathy for the Panchen Lama, revealing that he knew the truth of the matter. Even though the Panchen Lama occupies a higher position in the Tibetan hierarchy than the Dalai Lama, the Chinese never had a hope of playing the one off against the other. No doubt Peking has come to realize this fact; had further proof been needed it was furnished by the Panchen Lama's arrival back in Tibet after an absence of nineteen years. Tibetans crowded around him in their thousands, and there were even reports of people being injured and killed in the crush. In the Tsuglagkhang the Panchen Lama made an offering of rice on three tiers of silver trays as his gift to the shrine. He then prostrated himself before the statue of Jo Rinpoche and loudly and clearly prayed for the Dalai Lama's return, voicing a sentiment that regained him the Tibetan people's veneration: "There is but one man who is worthy to sit on this throne—His Holiness the Dalai Lama, Tenzin Gyatso." He then spoke to the people, calling for tolerance from them and for believers and unbelievers to respect one another. The temple guards, the so-called *go nyipa*, the "two-headed-ones," the collaborators who had been in the temple merely in order to service the butter lamps, fled when they heard these words for fear of Chinese reprisals.

The Chinese, as they did also at the time of the Dalai Lama's delegation, had lost control of the situation. The Panchen Lama's return was clearly a shock to Peking's representatives, who thought that over the nineteen years they had sufficiently indoctrinated him to their way of thinking. The fact that the Panchen Lama had no longer been living in celibacy did not diminish the Tibetans' delight at his homecoming. He had another enthusiastic reception at his monastery of Tashilhünpo, where a new palace had been built for him.

Looking back on all the stories about the Panchen Lama's alleged "collaboration," stories which have circulated for years, I feel certain that his visit to Tibet marks a further step on the road to better conditions. After all, the reports on his return come from Tibetans, and their words clearly betray their pride and their admiration for the Panchen Lama's courage in publicly supporting the Dalai Lama and religion. He is now universally revered as the highest incarnation living in Tibet at the present time.

30

FAREWELL
TO TIBET

Dawn was breaking outside; I could see the window growing lighter. Strictly speaking, a cockerel should now be crowing, I thought to myself. It would fit the mood. The first crowing of the cock . . . But there was not even a dog barking in the distance. The car was ready for our departure. It was cold, and the sun was slowly rising. We came to Kyentsal Lupding, the "Place of Welcome and Farewell." Of course, there were no tents there anymore, no cushions lying on the ground, and no tea or small sweet cakes. No one to place a white good-luck *khata* around our necks, to ensure the gods protect us and bring us back again in good health. Besides, our time of departure had been notified to us in terms of hours and minutes, and not as at the first or the second crowing of the cock . . .

I cast a last glance back: in the distance I could see the outlines of the Potala in the rapidly growing light, and I knew that it was for the last time. I was thinking of the words an aged Tibetan, whom I knew from the old days, had said to me, as urgently and softly as if he were imparting a secret to me: "Henrig, I rely on time. Time heals everything. So what do a hundred or two hundred years signify in our history or in our religion? We have survived over far longer periods in the past, and so far we have always salvaged our national character and our culture. I do not know what the future will bring, but perhaps people will one day inwardly reach the point where nations genuinely draw together instead of becoming estranged through misunderstandings. Perhaps, Henrig, you believe that things may work out rather differently, because people unfortunately are not all that peaceful. But let me tell you as a Tibetan—and I can only speak as a Tibetan—we have always been a peace-loving people and will continue to be so. We have never loved war, but we have loved our religion and culture all the more."

Once more, as so often in this book, a comparison forces itself upon me: my painful leave-taking from Lhasa thirty years ago, when I had still dreamed of spending my life in this "forbidden city" with its happy people, and the ease with which I am now leaving behind me all I have seen and experienced during this short period. Lhasa, whose name means "place of the gods," no longer bears any relation to that lovely name; looking at the ugly hutments and tin roofs, at the new buildings and their alien architecture, as they choke the few old quarters of the city, it is hard to believe that the gods would choose this spot for their seat on earth.

How good it would be to believe the aged Tibetan, and how necessary it is in our age, when money has become the measure of all things, to return to a more humanistic ethos. It is a goal that many young people all over the world are striving for. I regard the Tibetans as the most lovable people on earth—but I am far from idealizing them. For what one idealizes one cannot understand; one looks at a fictitious image instead of at facts. The Tibetans deserve to be understood. They genuinely possess a multitude of marvelous qualities, but also a multitude of special idiosyncrasies; all these have to be added up if one wants to do them justice. Preconceived ideas should be put aside whenever one approaches different people, and no credence should be given to generalizations. It seems to me that the Tibetans have long had to suffer from just that. I do not presume to claim that I know them down to the last detail, or can see through them, but I know that they are particularly lovable and cheerful and hardworking, and far more honest in their fashion than a lot of Europeans and Americans, not to mention the Chinese.

Our car was rattling along. It was icy cold. I recognized the outlines of the ancient Nethang temple with the well-preserved walls enclosing it. In the face of this oasis of undestroyed beauty, I allow myself a vision which I dare not believe will come true—yet I cannot entirely abandon the hope that Lhasa and Tibet will one day recapture their fascinating atmosphere and bewitching charm. Needless to say, it must be under a Tibetan government implementing far-reaching reforms for the benefit of its own people, not the Chinese: a symbiosis of the ancient bright colors, of houses of timber and stone, brown, red and white, of laughing faces, and modern facilities which, of course, will result in a higher standard of living. The Tibetans, I would hope, will again be inwardly independent, living in peace with their neighbors, as they have done through centuries of their history. My vision reveals to me what might one day come about, if Tibet again became the dreamed-of land on the roof of the world, the land where youthful dreams find fulfillment. For all dreams begin in one's youth, and it was this country that supplied me with my dreams and furnished me with a goal for my life. Sven Hedin, the great Swedish explorer, wrote to me in Lhasa: "You have reached the city of my dreams . . ."

Would it not be marvelous if our young people could also possess their land of mystery and magic, their Shangri-la, a goal they would exert their best efforts to attain? They might stroll through the flowering hanging gardens below the Potala, as I planned them with Wangdü thirty years ago. The Tibetans are a patient people, they think in different time concepts, and the Dalai Lama himself has repeatedly stated that it is irrelevant whether it is the present Fourteenth Dalai Lama or one of the next incarnations that returns to Lhasa. Contemplating this, I can see that on that day of his return, unimaginable emotions will be released among the Tibetan population, emotions eclipsing those displayed on the occasions of the Dalai Lama's delegation or the Panchen Lama's return. I cannot imagine the Dalai Lama not being overwhelmed by an effusion of love and emotion. I can see the giant *thangka* of brocade and silk hanging down from the Potala, I can see thousands reverently and happily flinging themselves to the ground, I can hear their tear-choked voices muttering *"Yishi Norbu"* ("wish-granting jewel") and *"Om-mani-padme-hum"* ("jewel in the lotus"). *Chang,* the Tibetan barley beer, will be drunk, the beautiful colorful dresses of the girls will swish as they spin around, and the men in their fox-skin caps will perform their stamping dances. Perhaps the representatives of China, India, Pakistan, Nepal and Bhutan will again be sitting in the seats reserved for honored guests, and the pretty girls with their coral and turquoise head ornaments will pour the cloudy barley juice—just as I experienced and described it thirty years ago. No longer, however, in isolation but in continuous interchange with other nations of the world. Modern transport eliminates distance, and there will be a lively coming and going.

Visions, dreams, hopes. Permit me to indulge in them: I was granted the joy of spending seven of my happiest years in this country, and I cannot abandon my hopes.

The bare airport had a sobering effect on me; the world once more was gray. I felt cold. Only now, at the moment of parting, did I realize how the past few days had been interwoven with melancholy and painful experiences.

Even so, I was leaving the country—the country I had not seen for over thirty years—with a feeling, perhaps even the conviction, that changes for the better, from the Tibetans' point of view, are perceptible.

As we passed the Yamdrok Yumtso the first sandstorm sprang up, heralding spring, and the ice on the lake had melted. Both spring and thaw seemed hopeful omens.

For a last time my mind went back to those weeks in Lhasa before the entry of the Chinese troops. There had been a severe earthquake which gave us all a nasty fright and which was interpreted by the Tibetans as a bad omen. Yet not a single temple had been destroyed, and not even the skyscraper-like Potala had developed a single crack. It was left to human hands, guided by political hatred and fanaticism, to destroy Tibet's sacred buildings. Yet the ice-covered peaks surrounding the country are standing unchanged. No political system can ever destroy the "throne of the gods." Unchanged also, in the cold moonlit nights, is the cry of the wild geese and cranes as they pass over Lhasa. Their wing beat sounds like *"Lha gye lo"*—"the gods will prevail."

EPILOGUE

When I finished writing this book in the summer of 1983 I did not suspect that my fears and pessimism about the credibility of Chinese promises and concessions would so soon be proved justified.

Under the heading of *dzüma* I recorded the misgivings of numerous Tibetans I had talked to. I described the "Potemkin villages" I had encountered everywhere—in Lhasa, in the monasteries and in the temples. Yet in spite of everything I kept searching for signs which would keep alive the faint and tenuous spark of hope of a thaw. Now that spark is dead.

Distressing reports began to appear in the autumn of 1983, at first sporadic and unconfirmed. But before long the terrible news, presently authenticated by tourists, spread throughout the world. The so-called "thaw," upon which all Tibetans and all friends of that lovable nation had pinned such high hopes, had lasted exactly four years. I was reminded of what I had been told by so many Tibetans, now that those who had been too indiscreet vis-à-vis the Dalai

Lama's delegation or too friendly toward visiting journalists were the first victims: "... the people of Lhasa have a saying that the philosophy of the Chinese is to let the poison become visible.... Then lance it when it can be seen."

By now the number of authenticated reports is steadily growing, of horrifying but credible accounts of arrests on the most threadbare pretexts, such as black marketeering or smuggling. These pitiful condemned wretches had been seen on trucks, more dead than alive after physical and mental torture.

These prisoners were subsequently executed, not in Lhasa, the capital, but on the left bank of the Kyichu in a hollow behind the Pungpai, a well-known hill of sacrifice. One of the five political detainees sentenced to death was sixty-five-year-old Geshe Lobsang Wangchuk, a respected doctor of philosophy from the Drepung monastery. He had courageously spoken out for Tibetan freedom and severely criticized the occupation of his country by the Chinese. The Chinese have denied that Wangchuk has been executed, and I have in fact received confirmation from the Dalai Lama's Information Office in Gangchen Kyishong in Dharamsala that he is still alive and has been taken to a top-security camp, Tasung Khang, in the neighborhood of Lhasa.

No doubt by comparison with the tens of thousands of Chinese sentenced to death at the same time the number of Tibetans was small—but how can one apply arithmetic to human lives, when each single killing is one too many? Besides, every execution further diminishes the chances of survival of the small Tibetan minority. My pessimistic view, frequently stated, that politicians always apply a double yardstick, and that economic and material interests invariably override humane and cultural considerations, is borne out by the following quotations from the world press on the subject of Tibet.

The reputable *Neue Züricher Zeitung* said on September 29, 1983:

Official Chinese quarters, according to the Dalai Lama's representative, are justifying the arrests on the grounds that action was being taken against black marketeers and persons without residence permits or without food ration cards. It had, however, been admitted that those under arrest also included political activists. The Chinese authorities had allowed it to be understood that some of those under arrest would have to expect the death penalty.

The *Liechtenstein Vaterland* observed on October 7, 1983:

> According to well-informed circles six Tibetans were executed in Lhasa last Friday for "criminal activities." Reports on hand as of Sunday gave no indication, according to information from Peking, on whether those executed were persons opposed to the regime.

The *Zürichsee-Zeitung* asked on October 11, 1983: "End of Liberalization in Tibet?" and reported "coup-like" actions by the Chinese in Lhasa, where five hundred Tibetans were arrested on August 24 and 28–29. Amnesty International in Bern immediately took up the matter and called on all Amnesty sections to mount an "urgent action." In this way thousands of its members throughout the world participated in that action. Countless similar reports, impossible to quote here, still lie on my desk. But in conclusion I should like to quote the internationally famous *Frankfurter Allgemeine Zeitung,* which, under the headline "Tibet Written Off," remarked honestly and compassionately:

> The Chinese oppressors evidently used a current "drive against crime" in the mother country to liquidate political opponents in

the Autonomous Region of Tibet. Tibetans in exile are certainly referring to "political executions." No doubt they know what they are talking about; so far their intelligence has always been reliable. Chinese attempts to conceal their misdeeds from the world have all been in vain. Yet hardly anyone in the West or among the noncommitted countries dares speak about it. The subject of Tibet is taboo. No one wishes to tread on Chinese toes, nearly everyone has been ready to spread a cloak of silence over events in Tibet for the sake of good relations with Peking. Afghanistan is almost forgotten, Tibet has been written off, the people of these two mountain countries are very largely or totally on their own.

A country with a highly developed culture has been written off by the world for fear that some lucrative trade agreement with China might be upset. For the same reason governments have carefully avoided receiving the Dalai Lama officially on any of his peaceful visits to Europe or America, while other radical political leaders are received with full diplomatic honors.

Is it surprising, then, that some young Tibetans should believe in the need to resort to violence in order to regain their freedom? So far the leaders of the Tibetans living in exile in the free world are still in control; so far they still believe they can achieve their right to freedom through peaceful means. To bring their fate to the notice of people throughout the world they stage "peaceful demonstrations" everywhere. In Zurich a silent peaceful demonstration of eight hundred Tibetans made a profound impression.

Where has our much-vaunted "progress" gotten us? Colonialism of European countries in Asia and Africa, rightly condemned, is fortunately a thing of the past. So is America's slave trade. But we have exchanged them for a neocolonialism which has swallowed independent free countries such as Tibet, countries perfectly capable of supporting and governing themselves, so that mighty powers should become even mightier.

Buddhism in Tibet never attempted to convert other nations, least of all by force. Tolerance has always been one of the virtues of this nation which is now suffering such hardships.

INDEX

Index

Index

COMING IN FALL 1998
FROM JEREMY P. TARCHER / PUTNAM

The White Spider

The Classic Account of the Ascent of the Eiger

HEINRICH HARRER

with a new introduction by the author

⌒

The White Spider is a timeless narrative that is the forerunner to such spellbinding books as *Into Thin Air* and *The Perfect Storm*. It is the definitive account of the first party to successfully scale the *Eigerwand*, the notorious North Face of the Eiger.

Harrer's record is a classic climbing yarn, influential to a generation of American adventurers. While examining the sheer physical endurance and skill needed to scale one of the world's most dangerous mountains, *The White Spider* also gives insight into the eccentric and frequently misunderstood psychology of the modern adventurer. Complete with photographs and a history of the doomed attempts which preceded Harrer's four-man party, this is a vicarious experience that irresistibly communicates the absolute joy and terror of climbing high peaks.

Tarcher/Putnam is proud to offer this edition of *The White Spider* with a new introduction by Heinrich Harrer. For anyone who has ever been entralled with the feat of climbing, this book is a lasting testament to human determination in the face of nature's might.

Seven Years in Tibet

HEINRICH HARRER

foreword by His Holiness the Dalai Lama

In this vivid memoir that has sold millions of copies worldwide and that was made into a feature film, Heinrich Harrer recounts his adventures as one of the first Europeans to enter Tibet. It is the extraordinary true story of how a young Austrian adventurer became tutor and friend to the Dalai Lama.

In 1943, Heinrich Harrer, a youthful Austrian adventurer, noted mountain climber, and skier, made a successful escape from an internment camp in India through rugged Himalayan passes to the Forbidden City of Lhasa in Tibet. From destitute vagabond, he rose to position of tutor and confidant to the fourteen-year-old Dalai Lama until their parting in 1950, when the Chinese Communists overran the country.

Seven Years in Tibet is a timeless story that illuminates Eastern culture, as well as the childhood of His Holiness the Dalai Lama and the current plight of Tibetans. It is a must-read for lovers of travel, adventure, history, and culture.

ABOUT THE AUTHOR

H EINRICH HARRER was born in Carinthia and raised in the Austrian Alps. He escaped from the British in India during World War II and fled overland to Tibet, where he and a fellow prisoner, Peter Aufschnaiter, won the friendship and respect of the Tibetans, and Harrer rose to become the tutor to the Dalai Lama and chief engineer of the country.

Aufschnaiter and Harrer were the first Westerners to gain the trust of the remote and isolated Tibetan people, who in the 1940s lived in a preindustrial world. After fleeing Tibet when the Chinese invaded, Harrer returned to Austria. He recorded his experiences in *Seven Years in Tibet,* which was translated into all the major languages and became a worldwide success and eventually a feature film in 1997.

Thirty years after his departure from Tibet, Harrer returned in the spring of 1982. In *Return to Tibet* he described life under the Chinese regime and compared it with the freedom of the past, when religion and faith were the central features and content of life.

In addition to his adventures in Tibet, Harrer has participated in several mountaineering expeditions and has written many books, including *Seven Years in Tibet, Return to Tibet,* and *The White Spider.* He lives in Liechtenstein and Hüttenburg, Austria.